DEVELOPING

YOUR

MARKETING

MINDSET

Amazon International Bestseller

Amazon Top 40 in the UK

Awarded New England Book Festival WINNER
Business Book 2025

Awarded International Impact Book Award
February 2026

Praise

Hands down, this is one of the best marketing books you will ever read!

If you want to transform your organization with effective marketing strategies, look no further than Leora Lanz's groundbreaking work.

George Bernard Shaw wrote that those who cannot do, teach. Leora has not only taught it, but she has also done it!

Leora's book brings together the classroom and the boardroom, offering critical insights to decision-makers, helping leaders navigate marketing challenges, and presenting real-world challenges and real solutions.

Leora Lanz is one of America's top branding and marketing experts. Her book will become the playbook for individuals and companies looking to amplify their branding and marketing efforts.

If a poor marketing strategy is a blunt blade, an effective marketing strategy is like a scalpel in the hands of a skilled surgeon.

Social media and artificial intelligence have brought us instant gurus, pretenders, gimmickry, and buzzspeak. Leora cuts through the noise and clutter with verve, erudition, and gravitas. The book is scholarly without being ponderous or pedantic and accessible without being superficial or artificial.

Developing Your Marketing Mindset challenges, inspires, educates, and entertains. This will be a worthy addition to your bookshelf.

—Dr. Jeffrey O, CEO,
International Hospitality Institute

It's clear from the start that Leora has poured years of wisdom into these pages. I can see this becoming a go-to resource for hospitality pros and beyond.

What I love most is how the text blends marketing strategy with real-world hospitality lessons—because let's face it, the best marketers do think like owners. The mantra of critical and strategic thinking is spot on, and I appreciate how Leora challenges readers to not just market, but to create meaning, build relationships, and think long-term.

The structure is great: practical insights, real case studies, and those marketing mantras that stick in your head long after reading. It's engaging without being preachy, and Leora's voice shines through as both expert and mentor.

I love that this isn't just for traditional marketers; it's for anyone in hospitality who wants to better understand the business they're in.

—Bashar Wali, Founder and CEO, This Assembly

WOW! WOW! WOW! This book is honestly amazing; I absolutely love it. I started writing down my favorite chapters, and then I realized I had basically written them all down! And I have to say, Leora's personal brand comes through so clearly—it's so her, and it's absolutely spot on. I always knew Leora was great at what she did, but reading this just made me appreciate her and her brilliance even more. I am so proud to know her, and reading this book left me feeling super inspired.

Reading *Developing Your Marketing Mindset: Real-World Lessons from Hospitality* feels like sitting down for a lively, inspiring conversation with a trusted mentor who's seen it all. This book is packed with real stories, smart strategies, and insights that spark fresh thinking and inspire you to see your work—and yourself—in a whole new light. It's an excellent reminder that marketing isn't just a department; it's a way of thinking, acting, and connecting, regardless of your role.

What really resonated with me is how it encourages you to understand the difference between critical thinking and strategic thinking—how to not only analyze the details in front of you but also think ahead with purpose and clarity. It pushes you to ask yourself, "What's my *why?*" and really reflect on the deeper purpose that drives both your personal brand and your professional decisions.

You're guided to see that a brand is so much more than a logo or a name; it's the promise you make and the relationship you build over time. The book challenges you to think like a marketer and act like an owner, blending creativity with accountability, always with an eye on building trust and delivering value.

And at the heart of it all, it beautifully reinforces that marketing is truly about relationships—the connections we nurture, the trust we earn, and the experiences we create along the way. This book doesn't just share lessons; it invites you to pause, reflect, and take ownership of your purpose. It's a powerful reminder that your story matters—and that with the right mindset, you have the tools to share it with authenticity, confidence, and lasting impact.

—Vera Manoukian, Former COO,
Sonesta Hotels; Former Global Brand Head,
Hilton Hotels and Resorts; Former President and CEO,
Denihan Hospitality Group; Former SVP Operations,
Starwood Hotels and Resorts Worldwide

Leora has put together amazing lessons that everyone can benefit from. My favorite principle she shares is, "Think like a marketer. Act like an owner." This principle emphasizes the importance of crafting marketing strategies that are not only creative and effective but also financially sound, aligning with the owner's vision and ensuring a meaningful return on investment. This is critical today as owners are seeing profits shrinking over time.

We don't just sell rooms, tables, or experiences; we represent the soul of the brand—the essence. And that essence is most powerfully communicated not through slogans or splashy campaigns, but through how we make people feel. It's in the human moments we create, the stories we invite guests to tell, and the emotional connection we nurture over time. Today's hospitality marketer must embrace the nuances that make our industry meaningful: the quiet power of sustainability, the rising expectation of wellness, and the importance of shared values. These aren't trends; they're the bridges to trust and loyalty. When we market with that in mind, we elevate the conversation, and shift from promotion to purpose. We transform transactions into relationships.

—Brian Hicks, President and CEO,
Hospitality Sales and Marketing Association
International (HSMAI)

I cannot recommend this book enough. As someone who works closely with future business leaders, I found this book packed with exactly the kind of grounded, practical wisdom we try to instill in our students.

The mantra, "Refine. Revise. Repeat," is now firmly pinned above my desk. It's a powerful reminder that good marketing isn't magic; it's a mindset—one grounded in iteration, hospitality, and constant learning.

This book distills years of classroom lessons and real-world marketing challenges into something refreshingly human. If you're teaching, studying, or leading teams that touch customers in any way, this is one to keep close by.

—Patti Brown, Associate Dean MBA
and Executive Degree Programs,
Saïd Business School, Oxford University

In *Developing Your Marketing Mindset: Real-World Lessons from Hospitality,* Leora does a masterful job of distilling the key strategies of hospitality marketing while bringing them to life through real-world examples and case studies. While referencing her professional journey and experience, Leora doesn't just lean on how things used to be or how they are today. She also looks to the future and highlights the marketing trends and challenges of tomorrow. In addition to Leora's marketing mantras in each chapter, one of the book's delights is the inclusion of her (former) students' voices as they share their hands-on practical experience implementing marketing strategies. The insights shared in this book make it a highly recommended read for all business executives—regardless of their job title or position within the organization.

—Chris Mumford, Founder, Managing Director,
Cervus Leadership Consulting

Developing Your Marketing Mindset is far more than a book about marketing; it's a guide to creating authentic, meaningful connections. Leora writes with deep understanding of what truly moves people—not just as customers but as human beings. Her lens on hospitality marketing honors personalization, emotional resonance, and purposeful storytelling, all while weaving in the wellness and sustainability values that today's most forward-thinking brands hold dear. For those of us who believe hospitality can be a force for good—nurturing body, mind, spirit, and place—this book offers both inspiration and practical direction.

—Susie Arnett, Director of Wellness Programming,
Six Senses

I've had the great pleasure of working with Leora through her marketing classes at Boston University, where I've witnessed firsthand how she guides students, and my businesses, to think differently—smarter, sharper, and more strategically. She has an amazing ability to challenge assumptions while making you feel inspired and supported. *Developing Your Marketing Mindset* brings that same energy to life.

This book is awesome, with real-world lessons rooted in hospitality, but its wisdom stretches far beyond the industry. Leora breaks down what it truly means to "think like a marketer and act like an owner"—a mindset that every leader, entrepreneur, or operator should embrace; I certainly try. Her insights are grounded, practical, and thought-provoking, with stories that feel both familiar and fresh. Whether you're running a restaurant, leading a team, or launching a brand, this book will shift the way you see your business and your role in it.

Leora's vision and approach have helped my team see new angles and opportunities we might have otherwise missed. I know they'll do the same for you.

—Andy Husbands, Pitmaster/Owner/Author,
The Smoke Shop BBQ

I've had the great fortune to work alongside Leora on numerous projects and got to witness her marketing approach and brilliance firsthand. Reading through this book gives you full access to her winning mindset and business mantras and provides you with the insights and examples from which you can readily build and shape your own success. The wisdom she shares in these pages may be rooted in hospitality, but the lessons and their endless benefits are universal.

—Gary Leopold, Founding Partner,
Prism Advisory Group; Former Chairman and
President of marketing firm ISM; and
President of the MAGNET Global Agency Network

With warmth, clarity, and real-world insight, *Developing Your Marketing Mindset* shows that marketing isn't just about selling; it's about storytelling, alignment, and impact. I was especially inspired by student case studies that reveal creative, values-driven approaches to real-world challenges. At the Center for Responsible Hospitality, we believe that doing good and doing well go hand in hand. Leora makes the case that marketing with heart, and with a clear why, is both a business imperative and a pathway to impact. This book brings that vision to life, inviting all of us to think like marketers, act with intention, and lead with hospitality.

—Rebecca Ruf, Founder and CEO,
Center for Responsible Hospitality

In *Developing Your Marketing Mindset: Real-World Lessons from Hospitality*, Leora delivers a timely and essential guide for those of us committed to advancing wellness, sustainability, community, and authentic connection in travel and tourism. Her message—that marketing is not just about selling but about serving with empathy and intention—aligns beautifully with our values at WITT. This book challenges readers to think beyond transactions—to see marketing as a powerful expression of hospitality. With deep wisdom, actionable insights, and heartfelt examples, Leora empowers professionals across our industry to embed wellness and responsibility into customer touchpoints and marketing brand values. It's a must-read for anyone seeking to lead with purpose and market with meaning.

—Robin Ruiz, CEO (Chief Empathy Officer) and
Founder, WITT—Wellness in Travel and Tourism

With decades of experience at the forefront of hospitality marketing, Leora Lanz delivers a masterclass in modern marketing that transcends borders and industries. *Developing Your Marketing Mindset* blends real-world hospitality lessons with business-savvy strategy, providing actionable insights that resonate globally and bridge theory with practice. As a respected thought leader, educator, and practitioner, Leora distills complex concepts into timeless takeaways, making this an indispensable read for professionals at every level. This book will elevate how you approach marketing, customer experience, and business leadership in today's interconnected world.

—Andrea Belfanti, CEO, International Society of Hospitality Consultants (ISHC)

Developing Your Marketing Mindset grasps the essence of hospitality and its role in using marketing as a business differentiator. Leora is a skilled marketer, yet an even better teacher of the subject. Coupled with her instinct for hospitality, there is not a truer expert on these topics combined. This book reads like a well-journeyed story—strategic in nature, written with first-hand knowledge and examples to guide your learning. The book defines marketing, brand, and mantras while adding the tenets of hospitality throughout, such as in Chapter 1, "Think Like a Marketer. Act Like an Owner."

I highly recommend *Developing Your Marketing Mindset: Real-World Lessons from Hospitality* for anyone searching for a more in-depth understanding of the importance of hospitality in all functional areas, especially marketing.

—Patti Simpson, Chief Administrative Officer,
Union Square Hospitality Group

Clear, actionable, and refreshingly authentic—this book delivers real insight, not just information. Leora brings clarity and depth to the complex world of marketing, making it both approachable and impactful.... Really incredible. I will be purchasing several copies for my marketing team.

—Amy Silva-Magalhaes, Chief Operating Officer,
Ultimate Care Senior Living Management

Leora has created a gem of a resource here for anyone in marketing, hospitality or who just loves either. Part personal experiences, part case studies, all celebration of the intersect of this discipline within this industry. The stories, when combined with Marketing Mantras, Mindset in Motion, and The Scorecard, all provide actionable takeaways for each chapter that make for an even richer and more compelling read.

—Lorie Juliano, Global Head of Communications
and Public Relations, Sonesta Hotels

Leora's book reads like the ultimate guest experience: welcoming, thoughtful and designed with purpose. *Developing Your Marketing Mindset* isn't just a guide for professionals; it's a masterclass in hospitality-driven leadership.

—Scott Savitt, Senior Partner,
Chief Digital Officer, Connelly Partners

Leora's book is a very detailed analysis and recommendation for marketers on steps for success. What makes Leora's vision unique is that her experience is combined with her diverse network of marketers—bringing so much knowledge into one place. *Developing Your Marketing Mindset* is a must-read for marketers at any point of their journey.

—Pete Rosenblum, President, MAP360 Collective

DEVELOPING
YOUR
MARKETING
MINDSET

REAL-WORLD LESSONS
FROM HOSPITALITY

Leora Halpern Lanz

ISBN: 979-8-89079-340-9 (paperback)
ISBN: 979-8-89079-341-6 (ebook)

Hospitality Strategies Press

Table of Contents

Part I
Cultivate the Marketing Mindset through Critical Thinking

Part II
Marketing Yourself

Part III
What Does the Future Hold?

Foreword

Marketing is not statistics.

It's not click-through rates, dashboards, funnels, or the black hole that is "impressions." Marketing is remembrance.

It is the lingering taste of a moment. The unseen strand linking deed to consequence. The signature you leave when the lights are out, and the visitor departs.

Leora Lanz knows that. She does not simply teach marketing. She teaches meaning. Her work educates on how to merge strategic rigor with emotional intelligence—to take story and substance and match them with soul.

For over a decade, Leora has taught from the front of the class at Boston University's School of Hospitality Administration, shaping future leaders. With fire, not formulas. With stories, not slides. This book is a natural extension of that work. A syllabus, penned in ink and in the heart for anyone who thinks marketing can—and ought to—be different.

Developing Your Marketing Mindset: Real-World Lessons from Hospitality is not a textbook. It's a manifesto.

A reminder that marketing isn't pushing a product but inviting engagement. It's about resonance, not reach. It's a book that invites you to shift from transactions to transformation.

For although its origins are based on hospitality, its teachings are universal.

To anyone who works in insurance, retail, healthcare, or government—yes, government—if you work with humans, then this book was created for you. Because human connection is not limited to an industry. Empathy knows no classification. A marketing mindset isn't tied to brands that have a concierge counter. It's a mindset that any fearless leader can adopt when they dare to ask themselves, "How do I make people feel?"

And we require that today more than ever.

It's a seven-second scroll world. There's a fatigue of attention. Brand has turned performative. Content is ephemeral. Campaigns are swallowed by a vortex of likes and skips.

Leora's solution is not to pursue the noise, but to make noise. Craft brands that stand out not with volume, but with voice. That is what this book provides: focus amidst a sea of noise.

It is also practical.

From digital presence and personalization to trust and brand development, each chapter provides you with means to not simply think differently, but behave differently.

The mantras are memorable. The case studies are actual. The work of the students is fit for a boardroom. And the chapter scorecards challenge you to stop, reflect, and make midcourse corrections.

Do not read it like a book to binge on. It is a book to sit with. To struggle with. To dog-ear and debate. Read it straight through or by chapter. Read it with engagement. It seeks to be in conversation with you.

Personally, I remembered the time that I first understood marketing. I was twenty-three, manning the front desk, observing a concierge salvage a ruined vacation of a family. Not with freebies, but with poise. It became clear to me then, and it remains clear to me today. Hospitality is marketing. Not the flashy kind, but the subtle moments. The real expectation of another's expectation. That is the point of this book.

That ethos comes to life through Leora. She balances decades of acquired experience with the pure, unbridled enthusiasm of students. That is the magic ingredient. It is not theory. It is lived experience. It is marketing education through the lens of real human beings doing battle with real challenges in the here and now.

This book isn't selling a strategy. It's selling a worldview. One where wellness and sustainability are not marketing tactics, but fundamentals. Where building a brand isn't a focus on volumes, but values. Where customer journeys are designed by intention, not automation.

There is no wasted space on these pages.

There is clarity.

There is conviction. There's a new type of marketer that's emerging here—the one that isn't just looking to be viewed, but to make a difference. So, if you are a student with a spark, a founder that has a nagging intuition that the status quo playbook no longer resonates, or a CMO eager to lead with a bit of a conscience, then this is your field guide.

Read it with a pen in hand and a fire in the belly. Since Leora isn't teaching you how to market. She's instructing you to make a difference. And that, my friends, is where the magic lies.

Bashar Wali
Founder and CEO, This Assembly

Introduction

Welcome to *Developing Your Marketing Mindset: Real-World Lessons from Hospitality*. In today's dynamic landscape, whether you're navigating a job, role, or running a business, cultivating a marketing mindset is not just beneficial; it's essential. However, what does it mean to "think like a marketer" and adopt a "marketing mindset"? Drawing from years of experience in the hospitality industry, I guide you through the fundamentals of marketing and hospitality, demonstrating how these intertwined disciplines can transform our approach and drive success. These are the principles I teach to students in advanced hospitality marketing courses. Do you possess the mindset that will elevate your endeavors to the next level?

Within these pages, I emphasize mindset, branding, and customer experience as essential for the strategic thinking that drives successful marketing. I recommend these chapters for leaders, business owners, and professionals who want to develop a marketing-driven perspective, even if they are not full-time marketers. This book focuses on developing a marketing mindset, relationship-building, and branding, which are foundational principles for marketers, business owners, and hospitality professionals. So, let's start with some building blocks to set the tone.

What is marketing? The American Marketing Association defines marketing as "the activity, set of institutions, and processes for creating, communicating, delivering, and exchanging offerings that have value for customers, clients, partners, and society at large."

In hospitality, marketing is about creating lasting value and engaging with those who appreciate it, extending beyond merely selling room nights or meals. Crafting experiences that stick with guests long after they leave is essential. (A "stickiness" factor is crucial.) This means creating lasting memories. Regardless of their role, every employee influences the brand's reputation through their interactions and work ethic.

Even if you're not in an official or formal marketing position, your actions and behavior serve as a marketing message about the guest experience and your hotel's brand. Recognizing that you are an ambassador for your employer is vital, so developing a marketing mindset that benefits your personal and organizational brand is crucial.

What is a mindset? The *Merriam-Webster* dictionary defines mindset as "a mental attitude or inclination, a fixed state of mind." It is the lens through which a person views and interacts with the world, influencing their thoughts, behaviors, and responses to various situations.

Possessing the right mindset can make a difference in your daily work and in your daily life. Here's a simple yet meaningful recollection of a service experience that lacked a marketing mindset:

> While walking through New York City a few years ago, I spontaneously stopped at a well-known women's clothing store to try on sweaters. The fitting room line was long. After nearly an hour, I was finally given a room. Like many shoppers, I had grabbed multiple sizes, hoping to find the perfect fit.
>
> Inside the dressing room, a sign on the wall conveyed to customers: "If you need another size, just ask our associates, and they will happily assist." Reassured by this promise, I stepped out to ask the two clerks stationed at the fitting room entrance for a different size. Instead of helping, they told me to leave the fitting area, take my items with me, and find the size myself. I asked if I could at least leave my dressing room set so I wouldn't have to wait in line again. After some persistence, they reluctantly agreed.
>
> This wasn't just a service misstep; it was a mindset problem. The store had written a promise to assist, but the associates weren't empowered or willing to deliver on it. One of them could have retrieved the

item with minimal effort, reinforcing a positive shopping experience. Instead, their refusal left a lasting negative impression—not just about them but about the brand. Frustrated, I left without making a purchase. And I haven't returned to that location since.

This experience highlights how a marketing mindset isn't just about promotions. It's about delivering brand promises, ensuring every touchpoint, from signage to service, aligns to create a seamless and hospitable customer experience that fosters loyalty.

In marketing, having a marketing mindset means adopting a perspective that consistently seeks to understand and meet customers' needs, leverages market insights, analyzes the competitive landscape and alternative customer solutions, and strategically promotes products or services to create value and drive success.

The word "hospitality" originates from the Latin word "*hospes*," meaning "host" or "guest," which ironically is also the root for words like "hostile" and "hostage." Hospitality refers to the generous and friendly treatment of guests or strangers. According to *Merriam-Webster*, it is defined as "hospitable treatment, reception, or disposition." In the context of the service industry, hospitality encompasses businesses that provide services to guests, such as hotels, restaurants, and bars.

Hospitality is about forging connections and evoking positive emotions. Hospitality is essential to the marketing mindset because it centers on building these genuine connections and creating the positive emotional experiences. It's not just about the product or service, but more importantly, *how you make people feel* throughout their journey.

Successful marketing hinges on mastering thoughtful, meaningful interactions that resonate with consumers on a personal level. By embracing the principles of hospitality, businesses can foster trust, loyalty, and a deeper connection with their audience—key elements of an effective marketing strategy that everyone should cultivate. Whether you work for an insurance company, a retail store, a bank, a car repair shop, a government agency (especially!), or any industry or business where people interact with others, developing a sense of hospitality is crucial.

Mastering the art of appropriate and effective interaction is key to successfully marketing yourself and your company. Everyone should cultivate a marketing mindset.

Over the years, I've encountered many students who say, "I'm not good at marketing; I'm just taking this class because it's required." Or "I won't pursue this as a career, but I know I should understand it for my company one day." Some even express skepticism, believing marketing is about embellishment, as one of my students in France once defiantly exclaimed. However, every professional activity involves thinking like a marketer. It's crucial for individuals and companies to understand and embrace this. Every interaction, whether with internal team members, fellow employees, or external clients, presents an opportunity to represent and market the brand, build customer preferences, foster brand loyalty, and encourage repeat patronage.

For a superior and positive work experience, we must all remember that we are marketers, whether we realize it or not. In the chapters ahead, we'll develop our personalized marketing mindset while shaping a clear understanding of what defines a hospitality marketing mindset. My journey offers insight into how mine has evolved.

My Journey

The career I've enjoyed thus far in the world of hospitality marketing has been eventful and immensely rewarding. It has been filled with both challenges and moments of joy. I've faced crises and challenging situations, including costly promotional campaigns that flopped, resulting in disappointed and sometimes angry customer responses. There have been incidents that attracted negative media coverage, requiring me to step into the role of spokesperson and deliver unfortunate news. From robberies and carjackings to other situations best left to the police, hotels (as I anticipated when I wrote my master's thesis many moons ago) are often the setting for unexpected and sometimes alarming events. From food poisoning and criminal activity by guests to protests over high-profile stays and even terrifying fires or natural disasters, the potential for crises is ever-present. Yet, working in hotel, restaurant, and tourism marketing has also offered creative promotional successes, international travel, and connections with a global network of intelligent, hospitality-loving, and like-minded professionals. It has been a career filled with invaluable lessons from both wins and misses.

When I began teaching, I realized I could articulate some of my favorite marketing philosophies as "mantras." Prior to that, I had never needed to define my marketing insights explicitly. Teaching forced me to distill the professional decisions I'd made throughout my career into coherent principles. Over the past decade, as I've shared my experiences in hospitality and marketing with students, I've found myself repeating certain phrases and philosophies so often that they've become integral to my vocabulary. I realized I was speaking a specific language, and I now have the privilege of teaching it.

My Passion for Hospitality

As a teenager, I dreamed of becoming an on-air anchor for NBC's *Today* show, inspired by the fearless journalism of Barbara Walters and Katie Couric's ability to balance serious news with lighter stories. I studied communications at Cornell University, intending to pursue a career in broadcast journalism, and even worked as a DJ at the college radio station. However, a pivotal college course in hospitality marketing taught by travel marketing legend

Peter Yesawich shifted my focus. It opened my eyes to strategic thinking in marketing, particularly in the hospitality and travel sectors, igniting my passion for global tourism and its diverse disciplines.

My undergraduate studies at Cornell led to graduate work at Boston University, where my thesis focused on crisis public relations for the hotel industry. This experience, particularly during the Dupont Plaza Hotel fire, which occurred during this time, highlighted the importance of effective communication in crisis situations. While in graduate school, I also interned at the Four Seasons Hotel (which had just opened), learning the significance of relationship building, understanding market segments, and collaborating with industry decision-makers and "bookers of business." This foundational experience shaped my marketing mindset as I recognized the importance of strategic thinking and revenue generation.

During my graduate studies, a class project turned into a job offer from the Greater Boston Convention and Visitors Bureau (today called Meet Boston), where I became the public relations manager. I coordinated city-wide promotional efforts, which enhanced my skills in managing a range of stakeholders and understanding the needs of various market segments of customers or third-party influencers, such as travel agents, travel writers, meeting planners, incentive planners, and more. My simultaneous work with the Four Seasons executives led to a position at ITT Sheraton Hotels in New York, where I was part of a dynamic team tasked with renaming, repositioning, and "rebranding" four significant properties in the city. This role deepened my understanding of international press relations and publicity for newsworthy moments, particularly during high-profile events like the 1992 Democratic National Convention, for which the Sheraton New York served as headquarter hotel.

In the late 1990s, during a hostile takeover attempt of ITT Sheraton by Hilton, I gained my first exposure to investor relations, which set the stage for a subsequent role as global director of marketing at hospitality consulting giant HVS. I supported the CEO and board of directors there while working with lodging operators and owners across the US and the Caribbean. This experience enriched my understanding of effective and integrated strategic marketing and the importance of relationship building. After fifteen fulfilling years in that role, I recognized the need for a personal change. However, the lessons learned from those roles continue to shape my marketing mindset today.

Marketing and Hospitality

Launching my practice, where I provided branding, marketing, and communications strategy and support to hospitality and hospitality-adjacent companies, marked an unexpected yet critically important shift in my career. Running my business kept me keenly attuned to client needs while deepening my understanding of the expansive world of hospitality marketing. My work involved marketing planning, sales training, social media advisory, writing and ghostwriting, creating podcasts, media engagement, strategic messaging, partnership facilitation, overall branding strategies, and more.

I had the privilege of collaborating with experts across various hospitality specializations, including leadership consulting, corporate governance, sustainability, wellness, hotel investment, real estate development in regions such as the Caribbean, Cuba, Central and South America, and India, as well as a hotel owners association. As you'll read throughout these pages, the direct connections and work I accomplished with hotel owners led me to retain the creativity and effectiveness of a marketer and the actions and mindset of the owner.

Each step of this unexpected journey brought challenges and opportunities that enriched my understanding of marketing and communications. I honed my skills in identifying innovative strategies, analyzing market trends, and crafting compelling campaigns that resonate with diverse audiences. These experiences form the foundation of the expertise I now impart to students as associate professor of the practice at my graduate alma mater, Boston University (BU), in the School of Hospitality Administration (SHA). I have realized that the lessons I've learned from my career experiences can guide others in any business. I hope some elements resonate and can be interpreted to help you, the reader, with professional situations you may face.

Joining the faculty at SHA in January 2015 was a "happy accident," as it introduced me to the joy of inspiring the next generation of passionate hospitality leaders and marketers. The intrinsic reward of teaching and mentoring students and creating courses that allow them to work with current hospitality businesses in real time also keeps me engaged and continually learning. This ongoing connection with the industry and my global network of colleagues and friends are vital for staying impactful and purposeful.

Teaching students to think critically, creatively, and strategically about the business today and its potential future is crucial for our industry's success. Marketing, an ever-evolving art form, demands continuous adaptation, innovation, and strategic methodology. I've developed courses, such as Digital Marketing Strategies for both graduate and undergraduate students and the senior-level Experiential Marketing class (formerly Advanced Strategic Marketing). I've also helped revise (and taught) our school's foundational course, Introduction to Hospitality. However, the experiential course has gained local acclaim, with Boston-area hospitality businesses eagerly seeking to participate. Selfishly, I utilize the course to help the local Boston community and contribute to its continued evolution and success. The students more than rise to the occasion; they graduate with pride in their work to foster meaningful hospitality business achievements.

Inspired by the exceptional projects my students have created, I wanted to assemble some of my lessons (learned and taught) into this book, aiming to encourage others to develop a marketing mindset. This book is not intended as an exhaustive guide, and certainly not a textbook, but a collection of insights, anecdotes, and key takeaways to inspire both non-marketers and aspiring marketers to act. I hope to provide some tidbits of practical wisdom to cultivate a marketing mindset, whether you work for a company or yourself. Through engaging narratives, practical insights, and real-world examples, I hope to empower you to approach business with an open mind, a spirit of innovation and thinking differently, and a willingness to learn from mistakes while fostering a successful and creative marketing mindset.

Back to School

And who better to contribute to this book than my former students, who have blossomed into remarkable professionals and executives in the working world, many of whom are rising stars in the hospitality industry. You will hear from several of my Boston University students, who are now making their mark across the US in diverse and fascinating hospitality roles. You'll also gain insights from my students at ESSEC Business School in Cergy, France, where I was blessed with a short yet incredibly memorable and wonderful stint as a visiting professor. These talented individuals, who studied in the IMHI (Institut de Management Hotelier International) program, have since embarked on impressive careers in hospitality across Europe, Canada, and the US.

When I share the student insights, you'll note that their quotes are directly addressing the chapter topic. I've also turned each student's commentary into a mini-marketing case study, indicating their class marketing project challenge and learnings. Please be aware that these mini cases are intended to subliminally teach us more as we go along. Please also keep in mind that the recommendations shared by the students and articulated in these mini-marketing case studies were not necessarily implemented by the client or business. Many were later, but what's shared here are suggestions based on research and best practices, as well as brand alignment, budget, staffing resources, or other parameters. These recommendations are indicated here to demonstrate critical, strategic, creative, and financially prudent thinking.

The pressing need for the hospitality and travel industries to address global and societal issues, such as wellness, sustainability, community engagement, technology and innovation, has never been more critical. As such, the demand for intelligent experience creators, critical thinkers, and strategic marketers is at an all-time high.

I am thrilled about these lessons' potential impact on marketing enthusiasts. I sincerely hope that by sharing these experiences, I can encourage other visionary marketers, whether in the hospitality space or elsewhere. These examples serve as catalysts for creative and strategic thinking. Even if your role doesn't explicitly involve marketing, I hope these philosophies and examples lead you to think about how best to represent your company and its mission.

This Book

I wrote these chapters to guide aspiring marketing students—whether in school or in the professional world—along with hospitality executives, service industry leaders, and business owners, who should inherently think like marketers. I hope that the mantras and stories inspire you to reflect on your business environment and approach challenges with a fresh perspective. Drawing from my career in hospitality and tourism, I offer a perspective filled with real-world examples that are easy to understand and relatable. These anecdotes serve as a frame of reference, which I hope will spark critical thinking and inspire solutions for your marketing challenges. If you're reading this, you're exactly the kind of person who will gain the most from the examples and insights shared.

In the hospitality industry, we welcome "guests." In senior living, we support "residents." In retail and service businesses, we serve "customers." Throughout this book, I may use the term "guest" interchangeably with "customer," depending on the context. As you read, I encourage you to adapt the terminology to fit your industry and interactions, ensuring the examples reso-nate with your experience.

This book is not an academic treatise on marketing prin-ciples, and as I indicated, it's not a textbook. Rather, it is a user-friendly and engaging (I hope) read that shares real-world examples of hospitality-centric marketing challenges and solutions to shift our mindset and con-sider new ideas. Each chapter stands alone while tying into the bigger message of how to think like a marketer. Each chapter is themed with a mantra that I share in my classes and concludes with a set of mantras or take-aways from those pages. I also conclude each chapter with prompts intended to boost your critical thinking and develop your marketing mindset.

While many reflections draw from hospitality, you'll also find examples from other fields. Use these best practices across sectors to inspire innovative solutions for your business, no matter your line of work.

This is a collection of cherished memories and anec-dotes from students who have applied the principles they learned in class to their careers and are now sharing them for practical application. The insights from former students included throughout these pages highlight the theme of each chapter, and all stem from a variety of inter-esting marketing challenges and hospitality examples.

This book is a personal souvenir of a decade of teach-ing, my passion for hospitality, and my experience in marketing. It is an expression of my desire to continue to contribute to the business of hospitality. Composing these chapters lifted me, and I'm grateful for the work accomplished in Boston with students, the work with students in Paris, and my accomplishments in New York and around the world. This book is a love letter to my Boston University School of Hospitality and my ESSEC IMHI students. Thank you, students; you keep me young and help me grow.

How to Use This Book

Each chapter concludes with Marketing Mantras, which reiterate several key takeaways. They also include Mindset in Motion questions to ask and apply the learnings from that chapter to elevate your work. At the conclusion of each section of chapters, a Marketing Mindset Scorecard allows us to keep track of our critical and strategic thinking skills for continued growth based on the takeaways from those preceding chapters. The scorecard allows us to self-assess, reflect, and evolve with a shift in thinking. This scorecard serves as a personal guide to help us think more strategically, act with intent, and approach marketing with a hospitality mindset. Our goal is to keep growing, keep learning, and, most importantly, keep marketing with purpose.

Marketing Mantras

1. **Understand that Everyone Is a Marketer.**

   Regardless of job title or function, every interaction you have, internally with team members or externally with customers, reflects on your brand and the company you represent. Recognizing this responsibility is the first step to cultivating a marketing mindset.

2. **Apply Hospitality Principles Everywhere.**

   Hospitality is about building genuine connections and making people feel valued. Whether you're in hotels, banking, insurance, or tech, adopting a hospitality mindset elevates the customer experience, fosters trust, and strengthens loyalty.

3. **Shape Your Marketing Mindset via Your Career Journey.**

   Whether classroom lessons, real-world experiences, successful campaigns, or challenging crises, each step of your career path refines how to create and communicate value. Embrace these moments as opportunities to grow and develop your unique marketing perspective.

Marketing isn't just about selling a product; it's about understanding people, creating value, and building lasting connections. As someone who has worked in the industry and now teaches and consults, I've learned that success comes from blending foundational principles with fresh perspectives. This book offers both a blend of real-world insights and practical strategies to help you think strategically, critically, and deeply—like a marketer. If we can strengthen our offerings to truly impact our audience's wellness or sustainability interests, or positively impact their community, we are marketing with deeper meaning and purpose. With that in mind, follow along as I introduce a few key marketing paradigms I teach in class.

PART I

Cultivate the Marketing Mindset through Critical Thinking

1

Think Like a Marketer.
Act Like an Owner.

"The objective of this course is to enable you to think like a marketer and act like an owner."

Every semester, I refresh my course syllabus with what I'd like to think are new and engaging projects. I update some of the class readings to ensure they remain relevant, impactful, and practical. However, one phrase in my syllabus always stays the same: "Think Like a Marketer. Act Like an Owner." This principle is deeply rooted in my career experiences, especially from times when I collaborated directly with hotel owners, operators, and management companies. It is an important mindset.

Early in my career, during my time at the Sheraton Hotels of New York in the 1990s—a decade marked by an eagerness to spend on bold initiatives—I often found myself in discussions with the finance and accounting departments. Marketing was frequently viewed as the department that "spent the money." I sometimes felt we could have justified even greater expenditures, given the substantial returns our marketing efforts were generating. This led to one of my first professional, conscious realizations, one of my first "lightbulb moments" (as I refer to them in class): We needed to shift our perspective from viewing marketing as an "expense" to recognizing it as an "investment." It was a concept I proudly championed, feeling as though I had uncovered a profound insight.

Throughout my career, I've been privileged to tackle fascinating marketing challenges in the hospitality sector. Many of my clients have been, and are, the owners of hotels, restaurants, and attractions. Owners are acutely aware of their budgets and constantly seek assurance their marketing initiatives will deliver a meaningful return on investment (ROI). They scrutinize every expenditure, requiring a thorough understanding of where every dollar goes and why—something I had to master as well.

The goal is to craft marketing strategies that are actionable, creative, and effective. The various communication and promotional ideas I've developed were designed to stand out, differentiating a hotel or restaurant from its competitors, setting a destination apart, or uniquely positioning an attraction. Some ideas leaned toward the quirky and attention-grabbing, just trying to create public relations buzz. Others were event-oriented, what we today call "activations" to encourage customer trial. Partner marketing and cooperative advertising were often employed to share costs. All efforts were integrated, meaning campaigns utilized multiple approaches to reach a diverse range of target markets through various channels.

Every idea had to be budgeted meticulously and prepared for scrutiny. Before presenting these ideas to owners, I tried to anticipate their questions and concerns. Boy, did I try. While the concepts were crafted for marketing effectiveness, they also had to align with the owners' visions and financial expectations. Thus, the mantra: "Think like a marketer. Act like an owner."

What is Critical Thinking? What is Strategic Thinking?

Great marketers and successful owners don't just react; they think critically and strategically. Critical thinking is the ability to analyze information objectively, question assumptions, and evaluate data before making decisions. It's what allows a marketer to sift through customer feedback, performance metrics, and industry trends to separate useful insights from noise. For an owner, it's the skill that ensures they don't make reactionary decisions based on a single complaint but instead look at the bigger picture before implementing changes.

Strategic thinking, on the other hand, is about looking ahead: anticipating challenges, identifying opportunities, and aligning decisions with long-term goals. While critical thinking helps make sense of the present, strategic thinking shapes the future. A marketer who thinks strategically doesn't just launch campaigns; they consider how branding, customer engagement, and competitive positioning will drive sustainable growth. An owner who thinks strategically doesn't just focus on today's bookings but asks: How do we position this business for success five years from now?

Both mindsets are essential because marketing isn't just about promotions, and ownership isn't just about operations. Owners who think like marketers understand the power of perception and customer loyalty, while marketers who think like owners recognize the importance of profitability, investment, and brand longevity. The most successful businesses are built by people who can think critically about the present and act strategically for the future.

Return on Investment Matters

It wasn't until I joined global consultancy HVS that I fully grasped the concept that hotels have owners. (Yes, I was young and naïve.) Before HVS, during my time with Sheraton Hotels, I knew ITT Corporation (now ITT Inc.) was the parent company of the hotels where I worked. They were "the owner." My role as director of public relations and advertising often required me to check in with corporate, given that I represented flagship properties in one of the most important primary markets in the world, New York City. As a public company, ITT scrutinized every piece of press and public marketing initiative I undertook, knowing that even minor actions could impact stockholder responses. I felt the weight of ITT on my shoulders, both metaphorically and literally, as their headquarter building was just a block from my office. The parent company's oversight was ever-present, requiring approval for significant expenditures and initiatives. At that stage in my career, I was not privy to all the high-level discussions handled by the director of sales and marketing, to whom I reported. My focus was on executing the work.

I vividly recall walking past the comptroller's office, feeling a twinge of anxiety as the accounting team frequently questioned our marketing spend. My thinking was clear: "Marketing is an investment, not an expense." I firmly believed we couldn't simply create weekend packages (or, as I now call them, "experiences") and expect guests to magically appear without any form of outreach or communication. The idea of "build it and they will come" was a myth.[1] It was crucial to reframe the perception of marketing expenditures within the organization, advocating for a view that recognized these outlays as investments with potential long-term benefits and revenue-generating potential. This mindset shift was essential for fostering a culture where creativity and financial accountability could coexist. By embracing this perspective, marketers position themselves to strike a delicate balance between innovation and fiscal prudence.

My experience at HVS quickly educated me on the realities of hotel ownership. Our clients ranged from individuals to companies that owned or operated hotels, often independent of the hotel brands themselves (though sometimes the brands were indeed our clients). Many of these owners were deeply involved in the day-to-day operations and actively invested in the success of their ventures. At that early point in my career, it was a revelation to understand that marketing recommendations were just that—recommendations. Owners had the autonomy to accept or reject them, depending on whether they aligned with their vision and financial objectives. This underscored the necessity of presenting marketing strategies that were not only creative and effective but also financially sound. The question of ROI was paramount: Do these strategies make sense for the product or brand, and will they yield a return on investment?

Ultimately, while it is our duty as marketers to present the most impactful ideas, the owners make the final decisions. Our role is to ensure that, regardless of the chosen path, the marketing recommendations are the best options based on our due diligence and research, balancing creativity with fiscal responsibility. This alignment between marketing initiatives and ownership vision is crucial for achieving a successful partnership and, ultimately, business success.

Think Like a Marketer. Act Like an Owner.

Marketing recommendations are strategic investments requiring careful consideration of ROI and financial prudence. Each proposal must undergo rigorous scrutiny to determine viability and potential returns. Whether advocating for a social media campaign or a large-scale promotional event, marketers must justify the expenditure and demonstrate value in tangible terms. We need the flexibility to make mistakes, but by measuring and monitoring, we can adjust course and ensure our efforts, time, and budget are used more effectively.

In my Experiential Marketing course, I emphasize this statement on Day One: "Think Like a Marketer. Act Like an Owner." If we're going to recommend a social media action plan, for example, the investment might be minimal. If we are recommending a large-scale event or series of events, a tradeshow booth, or a city-wide advertising campaign, for example, and the investment needed is considered substantial, we need to be cognizant of that and respect the owners who might invest in the recommended marketing activity.

Ultimately, the relationship between marketers and owners transcends the transaction. It should be a collaborative partnership grounded in mutual trust and respect. As marketers, we are strategic advisors, offering insights and expertise to support owners who may have their own intended direction. "Think Like a Marketer. Act Like an Owner."

Classroom Cases

The mini case studies from our classes that are shared below (and throughout this book) are reflections from some of my incredible former students. They manifest the principle that hospitality and marketing success hinges on delivering exceptional service and adopting a strategic mindset to drive business growth. This dual approach emphasizes the importance of viewing every decision through a marketing lens while taking ownership of the overall vision. Drawing from the diverse experiences of my former students from Boston University and ESSEC, these next few cases are examples of real-world insights and reflections from our in-class marketing planning projects. Together, we navigated the challenges of developing comprehensive marketing strategies, embodying the balance between creative thinking and responsible ownership. Their stories illustrate how embracing a marketer's perspective fosters innovation and customer-centric solutions while acting like an owner ensures accountability and long-term commitment to the business's objectives.

From Convention to Boutique: A Hotel Transformation

Student: Marut K. Raval

School: BU School of Hospitality Administration

Graduation: Class of 2020, MMH (Master of Management in Hospitality) Class of 2021

The Marketing Challenge: What marketing and communication are needed to help the Seaport Hotel in Boston tell its target markets that it is repositioning? In 2019, the hotel was set to decrease its room count through a large-scale renovation and create an intimate, boutique-like property, rather than the larger convention hotel that it had been since its opening.

Outcome: The hotel's plans were interrupted by the pandemic of 2020–2022, but the ultimate Communications Outline was a work of stellar planning and thoroughness. The student team ensured the communication effort reached B2B and B2C customers (individual travelers, travel planners, meeting planners, and more) and developed a campaign theme (Sea Change) to harness the messaging and ensure it stayed on brand and focused. One of the long-lasting memories of this project was the graphic timeline that was created to explain the messaging process, audiences, and strategies. This was a wonderful synopsis, a visual goal post, to show owners and the team how the plan culminates.

Marut's Insight: "'Think Like a Marketer; Act Like an Owner.' This is one of the most memorable quotes and best pieces of advice from our classes. It's relevant for any job. You need to think like a marketer to advance and develop your brand. For example, if you own a restaurant serving the best food in town, but no one knows you exist, you will have difficulty staying in business. You can't make a sale if you don't have any customers. Conversely, if you are managing the marketing for a restaurant but the budget is excessive, the business may struggle since not enough money is going to the bottom line. You need to find a balance to run a successful business.

"Although my team focused on the timelines and strategies for our communications plan for the Seaport's intended renovation, we had to think like owners and consider the operational impacts of a renovation. Therefore, our communication plan and phased timeline featured both long- and short-term expectations."

When I taught at ESSEC in Cergy, France, in the winter of 2024, I asked the seven teams of students to collectively select their (hypothetical) marketing clients. One team was asked to represent a chef of their choosing (either an established or a rising star chef); a second team was asked to select a Paris-based hotel (either legacy and five-star or newer and independent). A third team selected a restaurant to market (either Michelin-starred or nouvelle). The fourth team selected a wellness business or location. A fifth team selected a destination (already popular or a travel "dupe"[2]). Team Six could select a holiday, festival, or large-scale event. The final team could select an attraction (either a popular or more obscure one). Victoria Textoris's team agreed upon Fondation Vasarely, a museum dedicated to the works of artist Victor Vasarely, as their marketing plan subject.

Bringing a Quiet Museum to Light

Student: Victoria Textoris

School: ESSEC School of Business

Graduation: MSc IMHI Class of 2024

The Marketing Challenge: In this case, the challenge was hypothetical, though the museum is very real: Hungarian artist Victor Vasarely created an interesting form of contemporary art known as Optical Art. He emigrated to Paris, where he developed his signature style. In the 1960s, he established the Vasarely Fondation in Aix-en-Provence, a few hours south of Paris. The student marketing team enjoyed creating a plan for more awareness for this lesser-known yet highly interesting artist and the museum celebrating his works. The students discovered through their online and primary research that the messaging coming from the Vasarely was inconsistent in frequency, voice, and content; thus, the students developed outlines of plans to connect this beautiful art museum to families with children; adult groups, such as girlfriend getaways or couples; and other SMERF-type groups (social, military, educational, religious, or fraternal), including school and senior groups.

Outcome: Victoria and her teammates studied museum trends; reviewed the museum's strengths, weaknesses, opportunities, and threats (SWOT); and assessed the marketing of other smaller art museums in Aix, such as the Granet and Tapestry Museums, Atelier de Cezanne, and the Old Aix Museum. The team capitalized on Vasarely's use of bold colors to create fun messaging and eye-appealing branding for its website and social platforms, among other outreaches.

Victoria's Insight: "Think Like a Marketer; Act Like an Owner' is a powerful statement that combines two important mindsets for success in a business: strategic thinking with a sense of ownership. On the one hand, the marketer needs to be creative about how to present the brand, how to sell it (based on the company's value pillars), and how to spend money on strategy and all actions and services related to it. On the other hand, the owner must be conscious of how marketing impacts the company's financial well-being.

"My team had the opportunity to apply this concept when we were dedicated to promoting the Fondation Vasarely in Aix-en-Provence as our classroom exercise. To do so, our team had to first identify the Fondation's core values to help us provide a foundation for the strategy. Vasarely created Optical Art and became known as the Master of Colors. The key to achieving our strategic vision was to display creativity. At the same time, we had to remain cost-conscious, exploring cost-effective marketing approaches to meet the needs of the recommended strategies. We needed to optimize results while tightening the marketing investment.

"Our creativity enabled us to find effective solutions, notably by getting the most from already available resources. For example, my team adapted the offer already proposed by the museum to welcome school groups and attract families with children. In addition, we recommended enhancements to the tools it already uses, such as newsletters and social media, and developed ideas for strengthening engagement. Thinking about metrics allowed us to find ways to track the effectiveness of our marketing efforts and tie them back to business goals. This allowed us to demonstrate the value we bring, track the results of our marketing campaigns to see what is or isn't working, and adjust to maximize our return on investment.

"By thinking like a marketer, we can ensure our business strategies are customer-focused, creative, and data-driven. Acting like an owner ensures these strategies are executed with a sense of responsibility, financial discipline, and a commitment to long-term vision and success."

Reframing a City's Narrative

Student: Thi Thu "Hang" Nguyen

School: ESSEC School of Business 2024, Certificate in Advanced Hospitality Management from BU School of Hospitality Administration

Graduation: MSc IMHI Class of 2024

The Marketing Challenge: Hang and her teammates volunteered to tackle a truly difficult perception challenge for their class activity: repositioning a destination that generates both negative and positive vibes (and press) for visitors: Marseilles, France. This was not an easy task to undertake in an accelerated course. Yet, the team, which voluntarily selected their subject, was very passionate about putting Marseilles in a positive light. Each member of the team had favorable memories of the southern seaside city and eagerly wanted to adjust the tourism messaging and opportunities, authentically setting the record straight.

Outcome: This class project was not presented to an actual client, but it was presented as an outline of primary and secondary research, resulting in interesting observations. Though combatting negative media about crime, Marseilles was embarking on infrastructure renewal and offering a powerful cultural and modern culinary scene that is second to (in France), well, Paris. The team concluded visitors come to Marseilles after they've already visited Paris, so competitive cities included Bordeaux and Lyon (cities you might visit in France after you visit Paris first). The team also emphasized that Marseilles was a historic French city featuring ninety-nine protected museums and monuments. "If you come to France, then Marseilles is a must." They convinced me.

Hang's Insight: "When this concept was introduced in class, it really clicked with me. Thinking like a marketer means staying sharp, staying on top of trends, and understanding what makes people tick. It's behaving like a detective and an artist rolled into one, always looking for the next creative and worthwhile idea while staying true to the brand.

"Acting like an owner is about taking charge, owning your projects from start to finish, and making sure they really hit the mark. It's not just about ticking boxes but truly owning the results.

"In one of my other school projects, our team had to revamp a hotel's digital marketing strategy. I jumped in headfirst, conducted my research, and crafted a plan that was spot-on for the brand. Throughout the entire process, I felt like I wasn't just executing a job but really owning the project's success while still working effectively with my teammates. So, yes, the 'Think Like a Marketer; Act Like an Owner' philosophy sticks with me big time. It's made me more pro-active, creative, and results-focused in my work."

Having a student in class who was in a different course with you years earlier is always fun. I love seeing how these amazingly passionate, hospitality-curious people evolve into global and professional humans by the time they reach their senior year. John Barton was a fresh-man in my online Intro to Hospitality course, and I was blessed to have him join the fun in our senior-year mar-keting class together. Here's what John recalls about the concept of "Think Like a Marketer. Act Like an Owner."

Eco Pride: Promoting Sustainability in Food Service

Student: John Barton

School: BU School of Hospitality Administration

Graduation: Class of 2024

The Marketing Challenge: Levy's Food Service at the Boston Convention and Exposition Center (BCEC), led by Chef Kaeo Yuen, implemented impressive sustainability initiatives regarding farm-to-table produce, reusable serving utensils, and so much more. The Levy's team was certainly aware of the efforts and rightly proud of them. However, the team felt that promoting their sustainability successes could be adversely problematic, so they did not actively communicate them with clients or visitors. They did not want to "exploit" their goodness.

Outcome: The students' research proved that not only is it appropriate to market your sustainability initiatives, but it's also necessary. Customers are eager to support sustainable-forward companies and are even willing to pay more. The team recommended several ways to share the message using existing platforms, all with a unified theme. Channels included newsletters, on-site visuals and boards, social sites, and the BCEC's sales managers for effective word of mouth.

John's Insight: "For our semester project, we focused on providing sustainability-based marketing recommendations for a multinational food service operator working in a convention-venue environment. As we researched the ever-changing nature of the contemporary sustainability space while hearing from industry leaders, it became clear that many businesses at similar scales of volume were quick to think about marketing before taking ownership, and this, unfortunately, resulted in varying levels of 'greenwashing.'[3] However, Levy's was unique in its operation, having integrated sustainability long before it became a trend and before it could even measure ROI from effective marketing. Looking deeper, our team realized that their digital presence was not helping the marketing because it was nowhere near conveying the full sustainability story.

"One might assume that marketing one's sustainability efforts is regarded as boasting or inappropriate. However, our research enabled us to understand, and it became immediately clear how wrong and detrimental that assumption could be. The thesis of our marketing plan emphasized the need to market this information and reiterated that customers will gravitate to companies who are taking steps to 'do good in the world.' If they don't know about it, they'll go to someone else who is telling their story.

"As we presented to our client, I realized that *thinking like a marketer* was the driving force that helped *ownership make decisions and act.* I also learned if you implement adjustments to stay compliant, you should think like a marketer to help with internal and external communications of such initiatives."

The Digital Marketing Strategies class I created and taught required students to assess various online elements of a business's visibility compared to its competitors or other comparable companies. We look at the front-end user experience of a website and analyze its back-end effectiveness; we make recommendations for strong search engine optimization (SEO), whether through keyword mastery, blogs, or Google My Business optimization; we review paid search activities and email marketing; students will review the various social channels and online reputation management (ORM)—what users have to say through TripAdvisor, Yelp, OpenTable, or today, Reddit or Beli. The class provides an excellent assessment technique for aspiring marketers to review digital connectivity and presence. Master's student Vivian Feinstein took this digital marketing class, and explains she applies what she learned in her current role as a marketer and hotel owner.

Boosting Digital Visibility for a Fun-Focused Eatery

Student: Vivian Feinstein-Gough

School: BU School of Hospitality Administration

Graduation: MMH Class of 2020

The Marketing Challenge: Game On is an energetic and extremely popular sports bar located at the end of Lansdowne Street, adjacent to Fenway Park in Boston. The bar is owned by the Lyons Group, one of the city's premier entertainment and restaurant operators, and the entire class was responsible for reviewing the bar's digital footprint. The assessment included determining like-businesses and reviewing their online presence, too.

Outcome: The students presented as one cohesive team, with each group of students "passing the microphone" to the next to continue the conversation (a well-choreographed performance, as I refer to it). Teams of students examined the website and SEO, paid search outreach, online reputation sites, and all social media platforms. The goal of the project was to analyze the online presence and deliver three actionable recommendations for each of the areas of analysis. The Lyons Group director of marketing and social media manager at the time welcomed the recommendations eagerly and formatted the key takeaways into their action plan. Many of the student recommendations were implemented within six to nine months of the final presentation.

Vivian's Insight: "Currently, I wear multiple hats as a marketer, revenue manager, and partial owner of my family's hotels, which makes me acutely aware of the interplay between marketing strategies and business success. This perspective was honed during our digital marketing class, where a project analyzing a local business's SEM (search engine marketing, or paid search) and Google Ads strategy proved instrumental for me in my business role a few years later.

"When I stepped into the role as VP of marketing for my family's business, I had to first assess what we were doing for our marketing and understand our digital connection. I confronted the stark realities of outdated websites and minimal digital presence. Drawing on class insights, I understood that a compelling digital footprint is not just about aesthetics but a critical factor in customer decision-making. This, of course, required an upfront investment in marketing. However, as a marketer, how do you get an owner to approve your suggestions?

"Acting like an owner, I focused on metrics that matter for clear ROI and business impact. Metrics such as Google Search drove 10:1 ROAS (ten to one return on ad spend), which influenced my thinking as an owner. Convincing the rest of the family ownership to invest in digital upgrades, I needed to lay out how it would increase revenue or decrease costs. Upgrading our website and launching a comprehensive SEM strategy was needed to yield tangible results, such as a $14k investment resulting in $134k in sales. Effectively communicating top-line or bottom-line revenue allows decision-makers to be more willing to invest in marketing efforts. This approach ensures every marketing initiative aligns with our business's financial health and growth goals."

The diverse case studies presented by Marut, Victoria, Hang, John, and Vivian vividly illustrate the powerful synergy of thinking like a marketer while acting like an owner. Each student tackled unique challenges—whether transforming a hotel's identity, promoting a niche art museum, repositioning a city's narrative, enhancing sustainability in food service, or boosting a sports bar's digital presence—with a strategic blend of creativity and fiscal responsibility.

Speaking with Owners

I advise my students that when presenting recommendations, particularly those that may be uncomfortable for the client to hear, they must approach the situation with empathy and tact. The client's restaurant or product is often as dear to them as a family member; it's their "baby." Therefore, providing constructive and diplomatic feedback is essential, acknowledging the client's emotional investment in their business. Owners sometimes become so entrenched in their perspectives that they struggle to see the bigger picture. This is where the objective insights of an outsider can be invaluable. However, these insights must be delivered thoughtfully and respectfully. It's crucial to *think like the owner* with a clear awareness of the client's perspective. Understanding and respecting the owner-client is key to effective communication and maintaining a positive client relationship.

I remember a time when my colleague (and one of my dearest, life-long friends, Eydie Shapiro) and I worked with a resort hotel in the Pocono Mountains of Pennsylvania. We assembled a sales training plan for the in-house team and analyzed strategies to help with recommended future approaches. Fighting an awful cold, not feeling well, and certainly sounding uncomfortably sick, I, with Eydie's help, talked through each step and page of the plan we documented. We presented at a roundtable of six hotel executives. Eydie and I had rehearsed talking through the plan in a way that was sensitive and cognizant of their passion and emotional connection to the hotel. We didn't want to criticize. We wanted to show we were part of their team. We wanted to deliver observations respectfully, empathetically, and constructively.

As Corinne shares below, she had to put this sensitivity practice into action in our classroom presentations, too:

Intimate Encounters: Elevating Dining into Experiences

Student: Corinne Ognibene

School: BU School of Hospitality Administration

Graduation: Class of 2017

The Marketing Challenge: The Tasting Counter was in Somerville, Massachusetts, and during its heyday, it offered diners a very interesting restaurant concept. With only ten seats and timed tickets, guests purchased a multi-course, wine-paired meal, resulting in an intimate experience to meet other gourmand diners. The chefs worked at the open kitchen counter, where the guests were seated. Therefore, preparing the creative tasting menu was as important as the dinner and food itself. Foods were paired with all-natural wines, beers, sakes, or handcrafted non-alcoholic beverages. Lunch was a three-course event, and dinner was nine. Tickets were required and sold through the website. Who is the target market for this very different, high-ticket concept? How do we communicate to this audience, and what do we say?

Outcome: The chef and proprietor of The Tasting Counter, though admittedly a reluctant marketer at the time, welcomed cost-effective marketing ideas; it's difficult to justify a relatively big marketing spend when there's only a handful of seats to fill nightly. Suggestions included hyper-targeted, highly personalized outreach to foodies, individuals, couples, and small groups seeking an immersive and unusual dining experience, none of which was reflected on the website or social channels.

Corinne's Insight: "Our research suggested significant changes to align the brand with the expectations of its target audiences. Presenting this to the owner was nerve-wracking and scary—but it highlighted the importance of understanding the difference between internal and external perspectives. As marketers, we saw things differently than the business owners, who were too close to their concepts to see them as we did. This experience underscored the need to stay adaptable, listen to external feedback, and be willing to evolve."

Marketing Approach

By recognizing an owner's drive for return on investment, we can shape our marketing strategies and tools to connect with customers and contribute to the bottom line. When we blend this owner-focused mindset with a deep understanding of customer needs, every marketing tactic, from messaging to distribution, becomes more intentional, resonating with the customer on a personal level while delivering tangible value back to the business.

Strategy Process

So, how do we start to think like a marketer? What method do we use to navigate the situation or challenge?

- Begin with the situation analysis. What do we think is our marketing challenge? Define the product, service, or issue, and determine what we want to communicate to connect with our audiences. How are we the customers' solution?

- Identify the KPIs (key performance indicators) we want to achieve at the start. What do we want to accomplish? This way, we know where we are going.

- Research. Talk to people. Conduct primary research by speaking with individuals, conducting surveys, or organizing focus groups to learn more about the landscape, competition, trends, and existing models. Use legitimate sources to gather data and include them in our recommendations, ensuring we cite expert sources to support our findings.

- Identify our competitors and study them to learn from their strategies. What are our strengths, weaknesses, opportunities, and threats (SWOT), and what are those of our competitors? Perhaps look at the political, economic, societal, technological, environmental, and legal forces that impact the product (PESTEL analysis) to better understand our service and those of our competitors. Explore comparable businesses in other cities or around the world to gain additional insights. Examine their online presence and digital visibility by assessing their websites, social media, voice, and brand representation. Determine how they differentiate themselves in the market.

- Evaluate our website and all other digital platforms for ease of navigation and alignment with our objectives. Ask someone to navigate the site on a desktop, laptop, and mobile device. Conduct a back-end assessment to determine how Google ranks our site for ADA compliance, searchability, mobile efficacy, impactful links, and accurate information. Ensure we have a Google My Business page that serves as an additional "owned" site. Are our social platforms linked and robust?

- Identify our intended target customers based on this research, select three key segments, and prepare a market mix plan (three for my classes, maybe more in real-world scenarios). As the saying goes, "Never have just one egg in a basket." By targeting multiple segments, we mitigate the risk of a situation adversely impacting our business if one audience segment is affected.

- Determine the best communications and marketing tools to reach each customer segment, identifying three approaches for each group.
- Develop an overarching message to communicate our product consistently. Craft a tailored message for each customer segment, conveying the customer solution meaningfully to each audience.
- Allocate our marketing investment strategically across these initiatives to maximize effectiveness and ROI.
- Establish mechanisms to receive feedback and interact with customers, ensuring continuous engagement and improvement.
- Measure the results by evaluating program performance, learning from the outcomes, making necessary changes, and continuously improving strategies.

Spokes of the Wheel:
Finding the Right Balance of Marketing Tactics

Imagine a bicycle wheel, where the wheel represents the overarching marketing strategy, and each spoke symbolizes a different communication channel or marketing tactic. Just as a wheel relies on evenly distributed spokes for stability, a strong marketing approach requires a well-balanced mix of channels to effectively reach and engage your target audience.

Each spoke serves a unique function. For example, one spoke may represent social media, further branching into platforms like Instagram, TikTok, Facebook, and WeChat (a dominant social network in China). Other spokes may focus on public relations and press outreach, while others could represent direct sales, promotional campaigns, website optimization, search engine marketing, and traditional advertising.

However, attempting to leverage too many spokes at once can spread efforts too thin, leading to inefficiency and weak results. Instead, a strategic, focused approach is key. In my marketing classes, I advocate for selecting three key spokes at a time—allowing for a concentrated, high-impact strategy rather than a scattered, diluted effort. Businesses can allocate resources more effectively by homing in on a few core tactics, ensuring each channel receives the necessary attention to drive meaningful engagement and results.

To build a well-rounded marketing strategy, consider these five key categories or "spokes." Each represents a crucial set of marketing tactics. If you can share more, let me know!

1. **Digital and Social Media Marketing**
   - Organic and Paid Social (Instagram, TikTok, Facebook, Snapchat, Pinterest, WeChat)
   - Search Engine Optimization (SEO) and Paid Search (Google Ads, PPC)

- Email Marketing and CRM
- Influencer and User-Generated Content (UGC)

2. **Advertising and Paid Media**

- Traditional Media (TV, radio, newspapers, magazines)
- Outdoor Advertising (billboards, transit ads)
- Digital Display and Programmatic Ads

3. **Public Relations and Reputation Management**

- Press Outreach and Media Relations
- Crisis Communications and Brand Reputation
- Online Reviews and Community Engagement

4. **Experiential and Direct Marketing**

- Live Activations and Immersive Experiences
- Trade Shows, Events, and Sponsorships
- Subscriptions and Membership Programs

5. **Sales and Conversion Strategies**

- Direct Sales and Promotions
- Website and E-Commerce Optimization
- Loyalty Programs and Customer Retention

By aligning the right combination of spokes based on business goals and audience behavior, companies can build a marketing strategy that is not just well-structured but also adaptable, resilient, and results-driven.

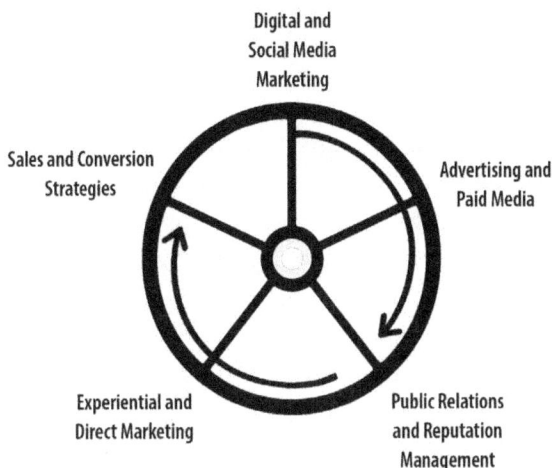

Think Innovatively

Gilles Henry is a French inventor. He identifies needs based on his life experiences and creates the tools to fill those gaps. He is the creator of Bastille, the first foldable full-size bicycle. Its versatility allows someone to carry it everywhere; therefore, there's no need to park it outside a building, leaving it open to theft. Henry is also the founder of the French brand Babyzen, which designs and manufactures high-end strollers, including the worldwide bestseller YOYO stroller, the first of its kind, compliant with size regulations for cabin luggage. He is a problem solver and disruptor.

I learned of Gilles Henry when I spoke with my colleague Marc Mazodier, professor and marketing department head at the ESSEC Business School in France, for the April 2024 issue of the *Boston Hospitality Review* (BHR: bu.edu/bhr). Marc also shared with me another example of a European company he considers a strong marketer because they innovate to provide customer solutions. "L'Oreal is a strong marketer. They spot trends constantly and activate them effectively. L'Oreal uses an AI-powered tool to detect new trends and inspire innovation."

"In my opinion," shared Marc, "strong marketing should occur when innovation meets consumers' needs."

I would add that when we meet consumer needs, in combination with great marketing, we strive toward success. The approach shared above emphasizes three steps to foster critical thinking in marketing: Thinking strategically and methodically, using a structured process with clear steps to guide decision-making; leveraging the right tools to connect with audiences, fostering meaningful engagement and dialogue; and creative and innovative thinking to develop solutions that effectively address customer needs.

As marketers, we must remember a key reality: Even our best ideas, backed by solid evidence, clear data, and projections of strong returns on investment, might not always be fully embraced by owners. At the end of the day, they are the ultimate decision-makers. Our role is to present the most thoughtful, well-researched recommendations possible, knowing that the final call rests with them.

This can be frustrating. A friend and industry colleague recently shared, "They implemented most of my suggestions, but not all. I can't include the project in my portfolio because someone might assume I endorsed the parts they added that weren't my ideas." While it's natural to feel disappointed when our work isn't executed exactly as envisioned, we must take pride in offering our best advice. Whether our recommendations are adopted fully, partially, or not at all, what matters most is that we continue to deliver value, stay professional, and maintain the mindset that drives success.

Marketing Mantras

1. **View Marketing as an Investment:**

   Recognize marketing initiatives as investments that offer long-term benefits and revenue potential.

2. **Emphasize Financial Prudence and ROI:**

   Prioritize financial prudence and return on investment in marketing recommendations, aligning with owners' vision and financial objectives.

3. **Adopt an Owner's Mindset:**

   Understand and respect owners' financial stewardship while presenting innovative and strategic ideas. Foster a collaborative partnership grounded in mutual trust and respect.

4. **Retain a Customer-Centric Approach:**

Focus on understanding and solving customer problems, engaging in two-way communication to build meaningful connections.

5. **Pursue a Strategic and Measurable Mindset:**

Start with a situation analysis and continuously assess and improve efforts. Utilize effective marketing tools and strategies by using a mix of channels without diluting efforts by spreading resources too thin.

6. **Combine Marketing with Innovation:**

Effective marketing combined with innovation that meets customers' needs leads to success. Remember, it's not about you; it's about them.

7. **Focus on Solving Customer Problems:**

Marketing should not be about your product, its features, or what it does. It should be about communicating to customers how you solve their problems. Engage in dialogue to show you understand and meet their needs and wants. It's not about *you*, but about *them*. Ask how you are their solution and how you can help.

Think Like a Marketer. Act Like an Owner.

By thinking like marketers, we harness strategic creativity to connect with our audiences, while acting like owners ensures our initiatives are grounded in financial prudence and long-term vision. Moving forward, we will delve deeper into the foundation of our marketing efforts by exploring the need to *understand our "why."* This next chapter will teach us why we should recognize the core motivations and values that drive our strategies, helping us create more meaningful and impactful connections with our customers. By clearly defining our purpose, we can align our marketing initiatives with our overarching goals, ensuring every action we take is purposeful and resonates with our target audiences.

Mindset in Motion

To cultivate a true marketing mindset, step into the shoes of an owner. Identify a current marketing challenge in your business. How would you analyze it differently if your investment was on the line? Consider your return on investment, innovative tactics, and how each decision affects the broader strategy. Document your insights and outline actionable steps to address the challenge as if you were the owner.

2

What's Your Why?
Brand Purpose and Values

Companies and individuals thrive when they articulate a clear why; their purpose goes beyond mere profit or personal success. This core meaning guides strategic decisions and aligns seamlessly with social impact responsibilities, often embodied by CSR (corporate social responsibility) and ESG (environmental, social, and governance) frameworks.

At their core, CSR and ESG frameworks revolve around ethical stewardship and sustainable impact, making them direct expressions of a company's deeper purpose—their why.

One forges deeper connections with customers, employees, and communities by rooting a company's mission in genuine social impact and responsibility to stakeholders. Ultimately, a well-defined why inspires authenticity, fosters meaningful engagement, and creates enduring value in a world craving purpose.

Start with Why

I'm a believer and fan of Simon Sinek. CEO of his namesake leadership consulting firm, prolific thought leader, and motivational speaker, Sinek presented his renowned TED talk, *Why Start with Why?*, in 2009 at the Puget Sound TED event. It's a favorite of mine to show in class each semester. Sinek famously articulates, "People don't buy what you do. They buy why you do it."

This statement says so much, doesn't it? Understanding *why* a company exists goes beyond just defining a mission statement; it often aligns with a deeper commitment to corporate responsibility. In today's business landscape, companies that successfully articulate their why are often those that integrate purpose with action, embedding ESG principles into their operations. A strong why inspires customers and drives corporate values, shaping how businesses contribute to society and the planet.

Simon Sinek's concept of why challenges businesses to define their deeper purpose—the driving force behind what they do beyond just making a profit. The most impactful brands state their why and manifest it through their actions, values, and marketing. Companies that have truly embraced their why go beyond slogans and integrate their purpose into everything from sustainability initiatives to ethical business practices and community engagement. Let's explore three brands that exemplify this principle—businesses that don't just market their mission but actively operate in alignment with it, offering *authenticity of their promise*. One standout example is the "outdoor loving" clothing and gear brand Patagonia.

Brand Examples

"We are in the business to save our home planet." This is a mission of environmental stewardship. Patagonia's mission revolves around environmental sustainability and promoting outdoor activism. They believe in creating high-quality products while minimizing their environmental footprint. Patagonia's commitment to social and environmental responsibility is evident in every aspect of its business, from sourcing materials to advocating for environmental causes.

Through marketing efforts and brand messaging, Patagonia emphasizes its deeper purpose beyond just selling outdoor gear. They aim to inspire individuals to explore the outdoors while fostering a sense of responsibility toward protecting the environment. This is their why. If making money, as Sinek explains, is the only reason for existence, the brand will not survive. There must be a shared value behind it—shared between the audience and the brand. Knowing your why will help build your brand, the foundation for a marketing approach, and your marketing mindset.

Here's another example: Patagonia's "Don't Buy This Jacket" campaign has challenged consumers to reconsider their spending habits and urged them to prioritize sustainability over unnecessary purchases. Patagonia launched this campaign on during the post-Thanksgiving shopping period in 2011 as part of its broader commitment to environmental responsibility and sustainability. The company wanted to challenge the culture of excessive consumption, which contributes significantly to environmental degradation. Patagonia sought to raise awareness about the environmental impact of overproduction and overconsumption by urging customers not to buy their products unless they genuinely needed them.

The ad featured a Patagonia jacket with the message "Don't Buy This Jacket," along with a detailed explanation of the environmental cost of producing each item, including water consumption, carbon emissions, and waste generated. The campaign encouraged consumers to consider the environmental footprint of their purchases and to prioritize buying durable, high-quality items that would last longer, thus reducing the need for frequent replacements. The mission was to promote conscious consumerism.

By aligning their brand with a meaningful cause, Patagonia resonated with consumers who share similar values and beliefs. Patagonia also has its Common Threads Initiative (encouraging customers to reduce, repair, reuse, recycle, and reimagine) and Worn Wear Program (to trade-in, buyback, or repair), among others, which are also a part of their history as a purpose-driven brand with corporate social responsibility (CSR) as a dominant part of its DNA. CSR is the core of Patagonia's values.

The success of Patagonia illustrates how articulating a compelling why can resonate with consumers on a deeper level, fostering brand loyalty and driving purchasing decisions based on shared values and ideals.

By the way, I'm a loyal fan of patronizing thrift shops and secondhand stores for clothing, accessories, and household items. The ability to repurpose an item gives it a longer life and allows me to afford something I could not purchase first-hand. Having enjoyed two multi-month stints in Paris in the last few years, where luxury items are respectably purchased in a multitude of second-hand stores, I can appreciate the French's regard for this aspect of sustainability. Thrift or second-hand can be luxury, too.

Okay, here's another brand to admire: "We use business to improve lives." TOMS is renowned for its one-for-one business model, where for every pair of shoes purchased, TOMS donates a pair to a child in need. This philanthropic mission forms the core of TOMS' identity and resonates strongly with consumers who seek to make a positive impact through their purchasing decisions.

By articulating a clear purpose beyond profit, TOMS positions itself as a socially responsible brand dedicated to improving the lives of others. Through their marketing campaigns and storytelling, TOMS emphasizes the transformative power of giving and encourages consumers to be part of a larger movement toward global change.

TOMS' commitment to social good reaches beyond footwear. With initiatives such as providing clean water, sight-saving surgeries, and support for mental health programs, each purchase of a pair of TOMS shoes becomes a tangible contribution to these humanitarian efforts, empowering consumers to also "do good" in the world.

By prioritizing social impact alongside profitability, TOMS exemplifies how brands can inspire loyalty and drive consumer engagement through a shared sense of purpose and responsibility. But what about the brands that weren't built as CSR-focused missions? What about a brand that may not, on the surface, appear to have a why other than products at a profit?

Let's talk Harley Davidson. "We fuel personal freedom and self-expression," delivering a culture of adventure and individuality.

Jeff Freedman is the founder of Small Army, which is now part of Finn Partners, a premier global integrated communications strategist agency. In his 2017 TEDx Beacon Street talk, *What's Your Brand Story?* (which I also show in class each semester), Freedman explains that every brand must have a moral to its story to connect, engage, and build relationships with customers. This TED talk also reinforces the concept of "know your why." Freedman briefly shares the Harley Davidson why as an example, and I've expanded upon it below for clarification:

Harley Davidson's why transcends mere transportation. Freedman explains that it embodies a "spirit of freedom, individuality, and rebellion against conformity.[4] At its core, Harley Davidson is not just a motorcycle manufacturer but a cultural icon synonymous with the pursuit of adventure and the open road."

The brand's story is rooted in the American spirit of rugged individualism and the quest for personal liberation. It represents the embodiment of self-expression and the celebration of authenticity in a world that often seeks to impose conformity. Harley Davidson's motorcycles are more than just machines; they are symbols of empowerment. They inspire a sense of camaraderie among riders, forging bonds that transcend age, gender, or background.

Through its brand narrative, Harley Davidson taps into a primal desire for freedom and self-discovery, inviting individuals to embark on a path of exploration and self-expression. It's not just about riding a motorcycle;

it's about embracing a lifestyle of passion, adventure, and the pursuit of the unknown.

I think I need to buy a Harley Davidson t-shirt right now.

As Freedman highlights in his TEDx talk, Harley Davidson's brand story resonates with consumers on an emotional level. It's a narrative that is not just about product features; it speaks to the deeper aspirations and desires that unite people. Essentially, their why is about inspiring individuals to break free from convention, to chart their own course, and to embrace the "exhilarating journey of self-discovery."

Each of these brand's distinct why—whether it's environmental activism, social responsibility, or a bold spirit of freedom—resonates deeply with their audience, inspiring loyalty, driving engagement, and fueling long-term growth. As Sinek repeats, "People don't buy what you do. They buy why you do it." So, think about what you're marketing and why it's important to your customers. Why do you do it? Why do you offer it? Why should anyone care?

Classroom Cases

At the ESSEC Business School, I asked student teams to select their hospitality and travel subjects for their marketing plans. The team assigned to market a chef determined they wanted to create a hypothetical marketing plan for revered French chef Yoann Conte. Chef

Yoann, was regarded as one of France's top names in gourmet cooking. He's a two-star Michelin chef; his La Table de Yoann Conte is part of the Relais and Chateaux group. ESSEC IMHI graduate Eva Kapoor shares her perspective about communicating Chef Yoann's why.

Elevating a Chef's Personal Brand

Student: Eva Kapoor

School: ESSEC School of Business

Graduation: MSc IMHI Class of 2024

The Marketing Challenge: Eva's team decided to learn more about and prepare marketing recommendations for esteemed French chef Yoann Conte. Chef Yoann was known for his human-centric approach to working with others and his focus on family. The team wanted to elevate his awareness and place him among the top names of gourmet chefs in France. He is a two-starred Michelin chef and a one-green-star chef who frequently appears on television food programs. The team wanted to market him as the "human" rather than as the "restaurant."

Outcome: The students reviewed social media for customer perception and considered many of the macro trends that affected the culinary world at the time—from technology to inflation and environmental initiatives to changes in French law. They compared Chef Yoann to others who had a strong online presence and identified target audiences and their needs and wants regarding fine cuisine experiences. This all defined the keywords suggested for use in communications along with initiatives to further enhance his "humanity" and "sustainable sensibilities." A social media calendar and other branding elements like the logo were created to soften his persona. A specific four-phase action plan was documented, covering the variety of content, social platform utilization, and live activation opportunities.

The team brilliantly recognized that by promoting his shifted and authentic why, he could diversify his activities and generate more revenue from collaborations, TV appearances, cookbooks, and other products—because the why is now about Yoann, the human, not the product.

Eva's Insight: "I can think back on the Simon Sinek video that explained to us how very few individuals truly understand the reason, objective, and purpose behind what they do. Our group's last task for the marketing course required us to promote a chef of our choice. We had to determine the customers' needs and the chef's needs. We were so enthused about the chef we had chosen that our group wanted to devise as many ideas as we could to market him. The ideas came flooding in, but we couldn't narrow it to one that made the most sense.

"At that point, we revisited what we had been taught, and we decided to figure out why we had chosen to market this chef in the first place. We selected this chef because of his goals, values, and accomplishments. We were aligned. At that point, we became aware that our perspective was entirely different. It was so much easier to determine how we should proceed. We understood the why and focused on it. We worked with it to market to customers with the same values. Determining what we should do to promote the chef more effectively became easier."

Branding a Fresh Hotel Experience

Student: Hoda Sherdy

School: BU School of Hospitality Administration

Graduation: Class of 2021

The Marketing Challenge: Motto was a relatively new Hilton hotel brand in 2021. It featured "micro-room" configurations and the hotels are in prime urban markets. The "Motto Commons" lobby space offered a place for community-building. There was only one Motto open and two more in the pipeline at the time of this project. Unlike traditional hotels, which intended to keep guests inside to utilize the hotel's features, Motto's mission was to encourage guests to explore the city they're in and "get outside." The posed classroom challenge was to help Motto further distinguish itself from the other Hilton lifestyle brands and help raise consumer awareness.

Outcome: Among the students' recommendations were creating local involvement opportunities for guests, connection with micro-influencers whose audiences were more targeted for the brand, and website and social media suggestions to enhance the overarching message of Motto's appreciation for community. Using the hashtag #MyMottoIs… allowed followers to personalize their Motto experience and express pride in the people and places that matter most to them.

Hoda's Insight: "What's your why? This is definitely the lesson that has stuck with me the most from my college days, and I use it daily. I truly believe that identifying your why is the most valuable tool a marketer or businessperson can use. As a brand manager in a small start-up, I'm involved in creative, logistical, and business decisions regularly, and I always ask my team, 'Why?' at the start of every meeting.

"Identifying our why, whether for a client video concept or a brand merchandise item, is always the strongest driving force. It drives our ideas to more creative levels and keeps us on task and streamlined because we know everything must come back to the why.

"I've started a quarterly why meeting with our CEO and key stakeholders to regularly assess the brand's greater mission and ensure every task, project, and technical goal continues to align with our why. When defining your why, I advise you to be direct and leave room for growth and adaptation. Marketing is ever changing, and businesses should constantly evolve, so it's vital to make space for your why to grow with you."

Revitalizing a Hidden Museum Gem

Student: Eugénie Foucher

School: ESSEC Business School, IMHI

Graduation: MSc IMHI Class of 2024

The Marketing Challenge: Eugénie was in two of my marketing courses at ESSEC, so she had two interesting projects: one of Paris's newest boutique hotels, Maison Elle, a brand extension of *Elle* magazine and the Fondation Vasarely, the museum homage to the work of Victor Vasarely in Aix-en-Provence. Eugénie was on the same team as classmate Victoria Textoris, who was introduced earlier.

In the case of Maison Elle, the challenge was for the class to assess the hotel's digital presence: its website, social media platforms, online reputation, presence on the OTA (online travel agency) channels, search engine optimization and keywords, paid search, and email marketing. The Fondation Vasarely assignment was designed to enhance the museum's marketing efforts to strengthen partnerships and event opportunities.

Outcome: Though Eugénie's memory here is about Fondation Vasarely, I want to comment on the Maison Elle outcome. The owner's representative who attended the final presentation of digital suggestions returned to ESSEC and offered a job to the student who could help implement the class's recommendations, which were simple, actionable, and important to elevate the hotel's digital presence.

Eugénie's Insight: "One team project was to assess and enhance the marketing of the Vasarely Fondation in France. The goal was to raise brand awareness through initiatives that enhanced consistent messaging. Determining our why was crucial: the Fondation believes in the power of art for well-being and for the mind. Its mission is to fulfill social responsibility by promoting art and culture, making it accessible to all. This clear understanding of their why helped us create a compelling campaign that aligned with the Fondation's core values, ensuring our messaging was authentic and relevant.

"On a personal level, starting with why ensures one's efforts are purpose-driven, fostering genuine connections and making a meaningful impact. This concept has also been instrumental in my professional journey, providing direction and fulfillment."

Enhancing the Appeal of Alternative Lodging

Student: Samantha Cooper

School: BU School of Hospitality Administration

Graduation: Class of 2020

The Marketing Challenge: Copley House is an affordable, short-term rental in Boston, offering furnished living in the Back Bay neighborhood. It is a collection of fully furnished apartments that can be rented for periods of time based on the needs of the guests. Guests can experience the cost savings of apartment living with essential hotel amenities, such as housekeeping services. The marketing planning aimed to strengthen the perception of the short-term rental product, emphasizing that the experience is "more than just a hotel" and is quite flexible to meet one's needs. The intention is that the marketing leads to more direct bookings for this type of lodging product.

Outcome: The family who owns Copley House listened attentively and receptively to the student's suggestions. The overarching themes of the recommendations were to develop strong and consistent branding to positively boost the public perception of this alternative accommodation and elevate awareness, to target niche potential audiences and increase the number of rentals per month, and to amplify the positive testimonials and guest experiences to encourage loyalty and return stays. If the Copley House's why is to have visitors feel at home in Boston, then share that purpose in the communication.

Samantha's Insight: "The question of why taps into foundational human emotion and motivation. Short-term and long-term lodging caused some confusion as it tried to distinguish itself from a traditional hotel as an extended stay solution. This confusion resulted in several important business challenges for the company: driving direct bookings, promoting off-season accommodations, and distinguishing nightly from monthly rentals.

"I learned when a business leads with purpose-driven marketing (the 'so what?'), a brand is equipped with the fundamentals to build long-term relationships with customers and stand out from its competition. The question of why acts as an effective marketing strategy guide because it's weaved with human emotion, impacts decision-making, and creates lasting impressions with customers. People will always remember how a brand or experience makes them feel."

The diverse projects undertaken by Eva, Hoda, Eugénie, and Samantha vividly demonstrate the critical role that understanding our why plays in effective marketing. Whether elevating a renowned chef's personal brand, distinguishing a fresh hotel experience, revitalizing a hidden museum gem, or enhancing the appeal of alternative lodging, each student harnessed the power of their foundational purpose to drive meaningful and impactful strategies. These cases also collectively tell us that knowing our why fuels creativity and strategic direction for authentic connections and long-term success.

Today, hotels, restaurants, retail, and other service businesses are hard-pressed to find staff who will arrive on time, enthusiastically, and ready to face whatever challenge arises during the day. Hiring individuals who arrive at work ready to service guests and share their hospitality is no easy task. Companies learned to market themselves through social platforms, particularly TikTok, to reach a potential workforce. Hospitality brands need to communicate their value propositions and core values to connect with prospective employees who are now eager to work for companies aligned with their values. Using raw and authentic user-generated content produced by employees can entice others to appreciate their place of work. (See more on Employer Branding as a Brand Extension in Chapter 4.)

Attracting Excellence: Hotel Employer Branding Strategies

Student: Chloe Brendlinger

School: BU School of Hospitality Administration

Graduation: Class of 2020

The Marketing Challenge: The Charles Hotel in Cambridge, Massachusetts, like many other hotels in 2019, needed to connect with potential employees to communicate the hotel is a great place to work.

Outcome: Chloe and her team delivered an employer branding plan that has since blossomed and serves as the foundation of many hotels' efforts to appeal to prospective employees. With labor in such high demand, hotels, restaurants, and all service businesses need to make the case for why their establishment is the best place for someone to work. What are the benefits to the employee? They also must stress how employees should take pride in their hospitality work; it's a career with many opportunities. Hospitality is not just a "summer job;" it is a wonderful career and profession.

Chloe's Insight: "With thorough research and comprehensive due diligence into the operation and an understanding of the culture of The Charles, our focus shifted to uncovering the hotel's core identity and purpose. It's essential to understand how the core values are interpreted by everyone at the hotel—from the CEO of the ownership company and the general manager to every associate, including the guest-facing doormen, front desk staff, and housekeepers. Everyone has a reason for working there and for working there as long as they have.

"The employer branding communication should resonate with that. By leveraging these insights and creatively sharing this message, we aimed to evoke emotions rooted in that purpose. We developed a marketing approach that humanized the hotel, characterizing it as if it were a human itself; we used images of team members to highlight their uniqueness and individuality and projected them collectively as a team, which embodied a sense of family. We identified their why and communicated it in our marketing efforts."

The discussion of why was intended to encourage students to understand their hospitality products and how to connect the messaging to the needs of their target markets. Often, students interpret the why discussion more deeply as a personal question to ask themselves:

"Well, what is *my* purpose? What is *my* personal brand about? What's my why?"

Sustainable Horizons:
Positioning a Destination for its Community and Environment

Student: Raegan Kelly

School: BU School of Hospitality Administration

Graduation: Class of 2024

The Marketing Challenge: In recent years, Boston's twenty-three neighborhoods have been regarded as leaders in sustainability initiatives with university environmental programs and green spaces or LEEDS certifications, among so many other endeavors. Boston's primary private sector and membership marketing agency welcomes individuals of all races, backgrounds, and generations to the 1,200 partner organizations. The marketing challenge was to instill a sense of responsibility in residents, travelers, and the Meet Boston membership to make meaningful changes and decisions with the sustainability of people, place, and planet at the top of mind—not an easy project. It was a very big and important challenge.

Outcome: The team developed a two-phased approach with three targeted personas, impressive data, and primary sources to assist Meet Boston in increasing this "be responsible" messaging. The Meet Boston executive vice president brought several industry partners to the final presentation and promised to incorporate the student themes and approaches into the forthcoming Boston Sustainability Committee Initiatives.

Raegan's Insight: "We needed to determine how to challenge ourselves, travelers, and current partner organizations to instill a sense of responsibility for sustainable travel. While the opportunities were endless, figuring out where to start was a struggle. Our team thought back to why. 'Why do individuals care about sustainable travel?' 'Why does Meet Boston have this responsibility to ensure sustainable travel?' Once we determined the why, the marketing journey fell into place. The why was our guide and laid the foundation for each step of the marketing plan. The why establishes your purpose and is the reason you do what you do. This enables a bridge for connectivity on an emotional level.

"However, discovering our why didn't stop with our marketing plans. It is integrated through all aspects of life. This lesson prompted me to question why I do the things I do. Why do I keep certain people in my life? Why am I pursuing my degree in hospitality? Why did I attend Boston University in the first place? Why do I want to eat healthy? I felt good about my intentions and purpose when I began to appreciate the why in everything I did. It provided me with meaning."

From the two last cases mentioned, we see that Chloe's efforts in employer branding for The Charles Hotel emphasized the importance of aligning the hotel's core values with its recruitment strategies, creating a narrative that attracts passionate and dedicated employees. Similarly, Raegan's work with Meet Boston showcased how a clear sense of purpose can drive sustainable initiatives and foster a deep connection with the community and stakeholders. These case studies, each unique in their focus, ranging from elevating personal brands and enhancing community engagement to promoting sustainability and strengthening employer appeal, demonstrate that knowing our why is the foundation upon which effective and meaningful marketing strategies are built.

Marketing Mantras

1. **Reflect on Your Deeper Purpose:**

   Take a moment to reflect on the deeper purpose behind your work or business. What core belief or mission drives you forward each day? Identifying your why shapes the way you act and communicate, resonating more authentically with the people you serve. What's your why?

2. **Know Your Why for Authentic Marketing:**

   Recognize that people are more influenced by the "why" of a company than the "what." This foundational understanding is crucial for developing a strong brand and effective marketing strategies. Knowing your why is the cornerstone of authentic and effective marketing. What is your company's why? Please, do not say it is "to make money." Of course, a business needs to make money, but that should not be our shared why.

3. **Embrace CSR and ESG Criteria:**

   Corporate social responsibility (CSR) and environmental, social, and governance (ESG) criteria are essential for businesses today. These frameworks guide companies in positively impacting society and the environment. Integrating elements of CSR and sustainability into marketing plans can enhance a brand's reputation and align with consumer values—as long as it's authentic. Customers can detect inauthentic values, which can be detrimental to a business.

4. **Exist as a Values-Driven Firm:**

   If your company isn't designed as a values-driven firm, identify a significant core value to both the firm and its audience and market the connection meaningfully and effectively.

This chapter has demonstrated how identifying and embracing our core purpose fuels relevant and impactful marketing initiatives. With a clear understanding of our why, we are now poised to delve into "The Brand" and "The Experience," where we will explore how to build a strong brand identity and create memorable experiences that resonate with our audiences.

Mindset in Motion

Take a moment to reflect on the core purpose of your brand or organization. What drives you beyond profit? Write your brand's why in one clear, compelling statement. Then, identify how this purpose aligns with your corporate social responsibility (CSR) and environmental, social, and governance (ESG) initiatives. Consider how you can communicate this why more effectively to your audience. This exercise will deepen your understanding of your brand's identity and help you create authentic connections with your customers.

3

The Brand and the Experience

Building an exceptional brand is about creating a promise that resonates at every touchpoint. In hospitality, this promise emerges through consistent, meaningful experiences. A clearly defined brand identity is core to successful marketing and how delivering a memorable experience cements that brand in the hearts of customers.

Understanding branding is foundational to conducting effective marketing. Branding establishes a business's identity, values, and promise, shaping and guiding our marketing strategies. We cannot begin marketing until we understand the product, the service, the experience—and the why. We need to understand the brand. And we need to distinguish that from the experience.

A brand is the strategic, emotional core (mission, values, visual identity), while the experience is how customers tangibly engage with that brand across multiple channels.

What's a Brand?

Today, every person, place, or product is a brand. A brand is the value proposition. It's the experience you have every time you encounter a product—digitally or physically—at any point of the interaction or customer engagement. It's more than just colors and logos. It involves understanding the emotional connection consumers have with a company. Marketers should comprehend and assess various aspects of the brand to move forward:

Brand Identity: The elements to consider here include the mission, vision, values, and personality. These influence how marketing messages are crafted and disseminated.

Brand Promise: The promise is a statement or commitment made by a brand to its customers, expressing the unique value and experience they can expect from interacting with it. It encapsulates the essence of what the brand stands for and what it consistently delivers, setting expectations for the quality, service, and emotional benefits associated with the brand.

Consistency: Consistency is key in branding across all marketing channels. Consistency of look, voice, tone, and promise. This results in a reliable and trustworthy brand for the audiences who care.

Strategy: The brand strategy forms a framework for marketing campaigns. A clear strategy helps marketers understand how to position products or services in the market and differentiate them from competitors.

Brand Equity: The financial value of a brand's strength in the marketplace is referred to as brand equity—the value a brand adds to a product or service beyond its functional benefits. It encompasses consumers' perceptions, associations, and attitudes about the brand, which can influence their purchasing decisions and loyalty. It is built over time through consistent brand experiences, positive customer interactions, effective marketing, and the brand's overall reputation. It can lead to advantages such as premium pricing, customer preference, and increased market share.

By aligning brand identity, promise, consistency, strategy, and equity, companies can create a powerful, trustworthy value proposition that resonates with customers at every touchpoint, driving loyalty, growth, and sustained market relevance. These brand elements serve as the foundation for every marketing decision, ensuring cohesive messaging and a consistent customer experience. They shape how you speak about your product or service, the promise you deliver, and how you stand out from competitors.

Consider a few insights and examples I share in class to help us shape our thoughts:

- Branding is about building relationships. Every touchpoint one has with a brand, whether digital, physical, or via word-of-mouth, builds the overall experience. Each touchpoint, regardless of how small or significant in the ecosystem of one's journey with the brand, is critically important. If a touchpoint is not delivered appropriately, it can harm and adversely impact the brand. Similarly, it can greatly enhance the brand, too.

- When a company, product, service, or social issue can brand effectively, it should meaningfully differentiate; it should be able to cut through the clutter of the competition and all other noise. The brand's strategy starts with identifying the positioning, determining the messaging, and even creating a visual identifier; this is developed by speaking with customers, conducting research and due diligence to learn and understanding how to deliver the valued experience of the brand so it's meaningful for the targeted market audiences. Ultimately, one hopes the brand is equally relevant for each of its audiences.

- The positioning encompasses the brand promise and identity and how the brand's values are projected to each target audience, with specific messaging through specific communication channels utilized by each audience.

What values come to mind when you think about Apple? Samsung? Starbucks? What do you think of when you hear the name Disney? Formula 1? World Cup? What values do you think of when someone says Marriott? Levi's? Prada? Louis Vuitton? St. Regis? These brands convey distinct and powerful meanings to all their customers. While people may stay in Marriotts for various reasons, there are common brand values each audience finds important for staying loyal to the brand. Brands should be authentic while remaining durable, "evolvable," and meaningful. It is the customer's "go-to." It's the customer's solution.

We market brands.

Therefore, building a strong brand is not just about creating a flashy logo or catchy tagline; it's about crafting a compelling narrative, fostering emotional connections, and delivering consistent, memorable experiences.

What's the Experience?

The Experience =
Physical + Digital + Emotional Interactions

Do you have a "Hilton experience" each time you stay at one of their thirty-plus sub-branded properties? Do you frequent Chipotle, as my sons do, and experience dining consistency? How does a hotel, restaurant, attraction, or festival continue to grow and evolve while retaining the reliable trust among fans, resulting in valuable brand loyalty? Think about a favorite bar you've frequented or an event you've attended, one you go to regularly. What constitutes their engagement with you and keeps bringing you back? How is your experience meaningful each time you frequent the business? What do they do right to ensure you have a reliable brand experience? What is their physical connection with you? How do they digitally connect? How do you feel when you connect with your favorite brands?

There are onsite physical touchpoints, such as the restaurant's ambiance or the retail shop's service. Businesses' digital touchpoints include websites, social media channels, and online marketplaces. How do these interactions make you feel about the brand? Are you frustrated by the clunky ordering process? Or are you confident in the seamless process of asking the customer service department questions on the phone or through a chat mechanism? These all comprise your connection to the brand.

For some of the companies I listed above, here are some thoughts about their brand values and the experiences they deliver. Consider the following:

Apple

- **The Brand:**
  "Think different."

- **The Experience:**

  Sleek, intuitive products that champion innovation and creativity, offering a cohesive ecosystem that seamlessly integrates hardware, software, and services.

Amazon

- **The Brand:**

  "Earth's most customer-centric company."

- **The Experience:**

  A frictionless, one-stop shopping environment, backed by fast shipping, personalized recommendations, and extensive product variety.

Starbucks

- **The Brand:**

  "To inspire and nurture the human spirit: one person, one cup, and one neighborhood at a time."

- **The Experience:**

  A welcoming "third place" between home and work, featuring consistently crafted beverages and an inviting atmosphere that fosters community.

Disney

- **The Brand:**

  "To create happiness by providing the finest in entertainment for people of all ages, everywhere."

- **The Experience:**

  Immersive worlds, from theme parks to films, where storytelling and enchantment delight guests and reinforce the sense of Disney magic.

These brands strive to ensure that every aspect of the experience reflects their values, identity, and promise. These brands create seamless and memorable experiences that foster unwavering loyalty by meticulously orchestrating physical, digital, and emotional touchpoints. As marketers, embracing this comprehensive approach enables us to design interactions that embody our brand's core values and deeply resonate with our audience, ensuring lasting engagement and trust (more on this topic later).

Authenticity, Promise, and Delivery

I was fortunate to have the opportunity to speak with Julie Freeman for the April 2024 issue of the *Boston Hospitality Review*. Julie is the executive vice president of public relations for the Americas of MMGY Global, which has specialized in hospitality, travel, and tourism for over forty years. In our conversation, Julie shared with me her take on what constitutes a successful brand campaign and experience:

> "Marketing and storytelling have evolved and continue to do so rapidly because of today's technology and emphasis on social media. For brands to set themselves apart in the 'sea of sameness,' they must think outside the box and collaborate with strategic partners to leverage their messaging and maximize their reach. Effective campaigns aren't just about grabbing the consumer's attention. To develop an effective campaign, it must be relevant, meaningful, and highly creative for the target audience. Brands that truly understand and anticipate the needs and desires of their customers and speak directly to them provide real value. In addition, consumers will gravitate toward brands that are transparent and true to themselves. Brands need to live and breathe their mission statement. Authenticity is key."

Of the many lessons I learned during my Sheraton days, an important one was this: It is critical not to overpromise in any marketing message because if the product underdelivers, we have just shot ourselves in the foot. Conversely, if we under-promise and the product overdelivers, we lose a lot of customers who weren't convinced they should try us. How do we ensure we create a memorable experience and market it appropriately? How do we balance the marketing to equate with the operation? Hard work, so let's keep going.

Personalization and Data

Marketers cannot afford to adopt a one-size-fits-all mentality. Consumers seek experiences aligned with their values and individuality in today's hyper-connected and data-collecting world. Understanding this, we craft marketing messages, communication channels, and experiences that speak directly to the hearts of our diverse audiences. Today's technologies and social tools allow us to personalize. We need to perform better than, and before, our competitors do.

Personalization isn't just about addressing customers by name or recommending products based on past purchases. It's about infusing every touchpoint of the customer journey with understanding. It's about anticipating their needs before they articulate them and delighting them in ways they never imagined.

How can we personalize the experience and marketing? Cvent is a global company that offers event planning, marketing, management, and venue-sourcing solutions. In its April 2020 blog, it shared a few examples of hospitality brands that understand personalization and use it to better connect with their meeting-planning customers:

Virgin Hotels Chicago leverages customer data to enhance the guest experience. Research revealed that 40 percent of travelers stay connected via their smartphones while on vacation, with 29 percent using them to communicate with loved ones and 24 percent to gather information about their surroundings. In response, the brand developed Lucy, a free mobile app that allows guests to check in, make dining reservations, adjust room temperature, order room service, and more.

Instead of a traditional rewards program, Virgin Hotels introduced The Know, a preference initiative aimed at crafting exceptional experiences. This program promotes direct bookings by providing guests with the best rates, potential room upgrades, and highly personalized services. Guests can specify their mini-bar preferences, select treats for their pets, indicate food allergies, and more. The hotel then surprises them with small tokens and amenities tailored to their preferences during each stay.

Such personalization particularly appeals to groups seeking unique experiences, helping the hotel differentiate itself from other potential event venues.

Hilton Suggests connects with guests personally on Twitter. @HiltonSuggests elevated personalized hotel marketing by having engaged directly with guests on Twitter. The team actively monitored the platform for inquiries about recommendations in select US cities, such as Seattle, Miami, and Chicago. Members with firsthand knowledge respond with tailored suggestions, signing each tweet to provide a personal touch. Their recommendations encompassed everything from local activities and restaurants to hotel options, even pointing users to competitor hotels when necessary. With 120,000 followers and high engagement, the account enhanced

Hilton's reputation as a reliable source for a comprehensive travel experience.

Event planners often have numerous questions about venues and locations before finalizing their bookings. Consider establishing a dedicated social account to address event-related inquiries across all your properties. This can serve as a valuable resource for planners and increase awareness of the offerings available for group events.

Mercure utilizes a Facebook Messenger chatbot to help guests explore destinations. In 2020, surveys indicated that 40 percent of American internet users preferred digital customer service over speaking to a human on the phone. Hotels responded to this trend by adopting chatbots on platforms like Facebook Messenger, their websites, text messaging services, and Slack to enhance customer interaction and streamline bookings.

AI-powered chatbots provide relevant, hyper-personalized recommendations and services for both guests and event planners, creating a truly tailored experience.

AccorHotels' Mercure brand focused on immersing guests in their local destinations. In 2017, they launched a Facebook Messenger chatbot called Mercure Bot that assisted guests in discovering their properties worldwide. This digital concierge engaged with guests and helped them uncover local attractions. The bot effectively tracked location details and stories in a way that humans could not, and it leveraged geolocation to provide personalized recommendations, simultaneously collecting valuable customer data.

Investing in a chatbot tailored for group events can significantly enhance operations by increasing bookings, shortening the sales cycle, and boosting loyalty. Consider integrating the bot on group landing pages and sections of the website dedicated to event information. Many common inquiries from meeting planners, such as questions about space capacity, food and beverage options, availability, and technical specifications, are ideal for a chatbot to address, providing planners with instant, personalized responses.

The convergence of personalization and data-driven strategies showcased in these three case studies vividly illustrates the transformative power of tailored experiences in hospitality. These examples collectively emphasize that understanding and utilizing personalization is not just a competitive advantage but a necessity for modern hospitality brands. By deeply connecting with meeting planners, leisure, or business guests, brands can differentiate themselves in a crowded market, enhance operational efficiency, and build lasting relationships. The common thread across these cases is the strategic use of data to anticipate and meet individual needs, transforming routine interactions into memorable experiences.

Experiences Matter, Especially in Hospitality

Creating a compelling and immersive experience is fundamental, especially in service industries like hospitality, where fierce competition exists and lasting memory is key. The experience encompasses customers' physical, digital, and emotional interactions with a brand.

In hospitality, this means going beyond basic expectations to deliver personalized experiences catering to each guest's unique needs and preferences. This personalization differentiates a brand from its competitors and fosters deep, lasting customer connections.

While overarching segmentation helps tailor experiences to broad customer groups, true differentiation comes from recognizing and responding to individual preferences. This means using data and insights to anticipate needs, offer customized services, and create moments of surprise and delight that feel unique to each guest. Achieving this level of personalization requires a deep understanding of the customer and a commitment to delivering exceptional service consistently. In hospitality, where experiences are at the heart of the offering, this approach sets a brand apart and builds loyalty and advocacy among guests.

Brand Experience Micro-Moments: Physical and Digital Emotional Connection

While at Google, Jim Lecinski wrote the bestseller, *Winning the Zero Moment of Truth* (Vook, Inc., June 2011), a critical playbook for marketers who are looking to understand and leverage the digital landscape to capture consumers' attention and influence their decision-making process. A micro-moment is defined as a very short amount of time, usually one regarded as important in some way: for example, pausing for a micro-moment before replying. In the current age of micro-moments, these brief but precious times are when brands get to interact with the consumer. Each micro-moment contributes to the overall brand experience and should be memorable. No matter how fleeting, these interactions are crucial opportunities for brands to make a lasting impression. Whether it's the elegance of opening a Tiffany Blue Box, the ease of navigating a website, or the delight in a thoughtfully crafted advertisement, each micro-moment plays a vital role in shaping the consumer's perception and relationship with the brand. Thus, ensuring each micro-moment is impactful and meaningful in a world saturated with rapid interactions is essential for creating a cohesive and memorable brand experience.

Former student and teaching assistant Kim Kibler offers valuable insight into how physical experiences can create profound emotional connections. We'll also learn more about her digital marketing project for a fast-casual barbecue joint.

Adaptive Dining Ambiance:
Attracting Professionals by Day and Families by Night

Student: Kim Kibler

School: BU School of Hospitality Administration

Graduation: Class of 2018

The Marketing Challenge: One of Kim's marketing projects in college was to conduct a digital marketing assessment of Shed's BBQ, a Texas-style barbecue restaurant in the heart of downtown Boston on Bromfield Street, steps from the Park Street T station. The restaurant was the dream of brother-and-sister team Edward Wilson and Shawn Wilson. They devised "slow-cooked family recipes in a quick-service environment" (Phantom Gourmet). How do we drive more lunch-time traffic to the Theater District? How do we drive more dinner traffic by connecting with families who reside within a walking radius?

Outcome: Shawn and Edward invited the class to enjoy lunch at the restaurant so we could taste the "Q" and witness the mid-day traffic and opportunities. It helps to know the food, the menu, and the atmosphere to create authentic posts and generate the energy of the place. The students talked about what we'd consider "the essentials," including claiming the Google My Business page and explaining why the mobile site's speed is critical. Assessing the website showed how the text was unclear and would impact the ADA (Americans with Disabilities Act) score. The students continued the review and suggested using Facebook groups to elevate engagement rates.

Additionally, students stressed the need to boost traffic on the online review sites, including Google Reviews and Yelp, and encouraged responding to comments to foster engagement. The use of Snapchat and geo filters was also recommended to capture local traffic at a variety of touchpoints during the consideration process. Ultimately, Shawn and Edward hired one of our students from the class to implement the recommendations, maintain social conversations, and post quality photography to reach the target markets.

Kim's Insight: "Opening a box containing an Apple computer is a distinct experience, evoking the excitement of unwrapping a meticulously crafted gift. This micro-moment, a hallmark of the Apple brand, transforms the simple act of unboxing into a ceremonial touchpoint projecting excitement, quality, and anticipation. The pristine white packaging, adorned with the iconic Apple logo, signals that this is not just any computer but a Mac, a symbol of innovation and design excellence. As the box lid gently lifts, revealing the sleek device within, it becomes clear this experience has been thoughtfully designed to reflect the premium quality and attention to detail synonymous with Apple. Many Mac owners cherish this experience so much that they keep the box, recognizing it as an integral part of owning an Apple product. Opening an Apple computer box is an experience evoking the essence of Apple's commitment to creating moments of delight and reverence for their users."

Other examples of memorable brand touchpoints and micro-moments from our classroom projects include:

Confusion to Clarity: Revamping a Convention Center's Website and Presence for User Success

The Massachusetts Convention Center Authority (MCCA), the operating entity of the Boston Convention and Exposition Center (BCEC), has been a frequent "client" in my marketing classes over the years because the former director, David Gibbons appreciates the thinking of the next generation and wants to absorb outside and fresh perspectives. The unusual structure of the MCCA (as indicated on its somewhat confusing website), with its other governmental and tourism partners in Massachusetts, means it often travels and works in collaboration with other entities to promote the state of Massachusetts as a desirable convention and meeting destination. One year, our students recommended, among various communications campaigns, a new and improved tradeshow booth, bringing all appropriate parties together under one roof so bookers of business who visited the booth at various tradeshows would understand the cooperative nature of all parties. This helped strengthen the MCCA brand by projecting a sense of teamwork. In this manner, all customers who visited the booth would feel the larger impact of the brand as a collaborative partner. The moment bookers of business enter the tradeshow booth, they feel the brand of Boston and its primary conference center.

Melodic Micro-Moment: Leveraging Music as a Memorable First Impression

In 2016, Newsfeed Café opened within the Boston Public Library, operated by The Catered Affair (TCA). The students were asked to create an opening plan to launch the café and to encourage passersby to enter, explore, sit, and sip. The students didn't want to just market the café; they wanted to create the experience so that entering, sitting, and sipping would project a specific ambiance, feeling, and distinct vibe. The students researched and explored competitors to better understand the nuances of this floor-to-ceiling glass corner location with its accessible newspapers and historic documents, as well as a podcast/audio cast studio visible from the street. One must enter the library to enter the café. The students suggested an early 1900s "jazz age" vibe with music piped throughout the common areas, including the bathrooms, and beverage and sandwich options to also align with the era. When presenting, the students brought a portable stereo (boom box!) to class to play the music and began their presentation with a soliloquy to put us all in the mood for this fabulous tone and setting. This created the brand experience for entry into the new cafe.

Aroma Attraction: Leveraging Smell to Draw Donut Enthusiasts

Union Square Donuts on Harvard Avenue in Brookline is an artisanal and delicious boutique brand owned by the Danoff family. Noah Danoff asked us to help with local community awareness because exterior signage and awnings were drastically limited due to town regulations. The student team, led by the culinary and restaurant passionate Jared Goldberg, among their many recommendations, suggested a donut-scented smell machine in hopes that it would lure passersby. Imagine that micro-moment of pleasure as you smell freshly baked goods, especially sugary or savory donuts, hitting your senses as you walk down the street. I know I would walk backward a few steps and immediately turn into the bakery. (I certainly was taken aback when I smelled fresh croissants each morning in the metros of Paris. It lured me to the kiosk to purchase and indulge every time I commuted.)

By designing engaging experiences, such as an easily navigable website, evocative aromas, or immersive sounds, brands can create meaningful micro-moments that capture individuals' attention and forge lasting memories.

Classroom Cases

Building on these foundational principles, let's explore how a few more of my former students, through the memories of their various in-class projects, have applied a deep understanding of the brand identity, promise, and experience to create impactful marketing solutions.

Distinctive Branding:
Elevating a Suburban Locale Adjacent to the Big City

Student: Micaela Yee

School: BU School of Hospitality Administration

Graduation: Class of 2023

The Marketing Challenge: Home to various cultures and ethnicities, Revere, Massachusetts, is an appealing destination for residents and travelers. The challenge of attracting more residents and visitors to Revere was explored on multiple levels, as the student team consulted with marketing specialists, realtors, and locals. Following extensive research and consultation, they gathered data and feedback indicating that an overarching theme is necessary to evoke positive emotions and increased visitation. Channeling their focus on marketing Revere as an experience rather than a destination, the team concluded that the city of Revere must create this theme using memorable taglines to elevate the city's brand image and emotional touchpoints.

The Outcome: The team delivered one consistent message for all its targeted audiences, which included young couples interested in moving to Revere and college-aged students who desired day-trip ideas from Boston. The campaign emphasized the area's natural offerings (beaches, parks, bike trails) and advantages of suburban yet semi-cosmopolitan living (proximity to Boston, ease of transportation)—all under an overarching tagline: *Rediscover Revere.*

The clients appreciated the approaches shared: Virtual tours online and even a virtual reality experience to explore the city, display ads on the rapid transit system for locals in Boston to see, specific micro-influencer collaborations for travel exploration (nature and the beaches) ideas, and the need to display more "pride in Revere" through social media. The city of Revere immediately began to execute the actionable plan, which was well-organized through a timeline.

Micaela's Insight: "Following the research for our project, our team transitioned to idea generation, focusing on creating actionable and budget-friendly strategies aligned with the city of Revere's brand. We were taught to consider the broader aspects of branding beyond visual elements, such as color palettes, taglines, and logos. We learned the importance of maintaining consistency in brand themes throughout our project work. The 'Revere Experience' is what we wanted to create and market."

Renewing the Legacy:
Breathing New Life into an Established Restaurant Brand

Student: Marut K. Raval

School: BU School of Hospitality Administration

Graduation: Class of 2020, MMH (Master of Management in Hospitality) Class of 2021

The Marketing Challenge: Earlier, we mentioned Marut's project to document the communication plan for repositioning the Seaport Hotel. Marut's other marketing project from his digital course involved an assessment for the premier national restaurant brand, Legal Sea Foods, which was founded in Cambridge, Massachusetts. The class enjoyed dining at the Copley Place location while we heard from the company's marketing director. The restaurant brand was established in 1950 and was now facing new competitors, particularly in Boston, where the expectation of seafood dining is exceptionally high. How can a legacy brand break through the music of new competition to remain a leading choice in the world of seafood restaurants?

Outcome: What I recall from this project is interesting: As the professor, my role included taming the students' enthusiasm for fresh ideas so as not to come across critical of the client. This was an excellent example of teaching the students how to delicately share recommendations, containing the excitement, and explaining how to take existing efforts to a new or different perspective. We wanted to compliment and congratulate the client for their work and emphasize that our goal was to provide fresh thinking and new approaches to their efforts.

Marut's Insight: "Marketing is supposed to create memories. Crafting curated experiences for a consumer is enormously helpful in cutting through the clutter of marketing messages because the target audience will remember those special events and moments rather than a 'typical' Instagram post or ad."

A comprehensive understanding of the brand and its experience directly informs the marketing strategy. A well-defined brand strategy serves as a framework for all marketing efforts, helping position products or services effectively and differentiate them from competitors. By aligning the brand's identity and experience with marketing initiatives, businesses can craft messages resonating more deeply with target audiences.

Just Around the Corner:
Driving Trial and Loyalty for Nearby Dining Experience

Student: Parker Doyle

School: BU School of Hospitality Administration

Graduation: Class of 2019

The Marketing Challenge: One of Boston's premier restaurateur-chefs, Andy Husbands, presented this to us. The newest barbecue joint in his portfolio (at the time), Smoke Shop in Somerville, Massachusetts, is located at Assembly Row near a shopping mall and near the (then new) headquarters for Partners Healthcare. How do we direct guests to the restaurant when it's not in the mall or inside the Partners' building? How do we create the experience and awareness of Smoke Shop? How do we inform shoppers in the mall and employees of Partners that this restaurant, though not visible from the mall or the office building, is just steps away?

Outcome: Chef Andy is one of the most candid and wonderful chef-restaurateurs I've ever worked with. He sets the bar high; fortunately, this student team did not disappoint. The team's due diligence included mapping the path to the restaurant from the sources of potential customers. What was needed was strategically placed signage and physical visibility, so prospective diners were aware this great lunch (and dinner) destination was just steps away. Digitally, the team also recommended how to use search engine optimization and Google Search to make the restaurant appear as "restaurants near me" when shoppers and workers look for lunch places to eat.

Parker's Insight: "A cohesive brand strategy is essential to maximize business profits. The brand must guide decision-making across all business platforms to speak with one voice and showcase one vision.

"My team (professionally, today) has led hundreds of branding, menu, operations, and design projects within the global food and beverage industry. Even when brand strategy is not a core project focus, it is central to our proposed menu, kitchen, and operating system, or store design recommendations. The brand is the business's voice and brings the spirit, personality, and culture to everything our client's business does."

Flavorful Conferences:
Marketing Culinary Experiences to Meeting Planners

Student: Kaitlyn Tran

School: BU School of Hospitality Administration

Graduation: Class of 2018

The Marketing Challenge: The Massachusetts Convention Center Authority (MCCA) owns and operates several event venues in the city of Boston. The MCCA sought to increase brand awareness and build stronger relationships with existing and prospective customers who utilize large venues for their social events or business conferences. The primary goal of this plan was to promote Boston as a culinary destination in response to the growing significance of food as part of the global travel and tourism experience.

Outcome: The research and approach included focusing on three personas: the event planner, the event attendee who has never been to Boston, and returning attendees. To best market Boston and the MCCA to these audiences, the team also used a three-pronged connection: Boston's innovation, dedication to sustainability, and growing dominance of female executives in the city's culinary scene.

This team's overarching message campaign, "Come for the meeting. Stay for the eating," was so well received that David Gibbons and his MCCA team implemented several recommendations as part of their subsequent initiatives.

Kaitlyn's Insight: "In our marketing class, I was introduced to Graduate Hotels in a lesson about leaning into a niche concept and going all-in with branding. Since then, I have been obsessed with the Graduate Hotels brand, even planning trips to just visit a property and work from the lobby. For me, it was about finding the 'missed market' and really diving into making it special—giving it a reason not to be overlooked. The appeal for these college towns is typically just the university, but Graduate Hotels has become another staple and place to be within these often-overlooked places. Really focusing on what makes the place special gives it an extra 'oomph' and truly one of a kind.

"I've taken this lesson with me for my career: not being afraid and truly going all in. It's not enough to just move forward halfway in any aspect of marketing, from branding to advertising the product. Don't be afraid to take extraordinary action and stand out from the competition. Find the details that make a product or service special and spotlight them. Think outside the box and try something new. It might become the biggest success."

Brand Re-Positioning to Stay Relevant

Some of the other hospitality marketing challenges we addressed in our classes over the years warranted us to modify the positioning and enhance the brand values and experiences while also appealing to new audiences altogether. For example, other class projects included:

- **The Moxy, Boston:** How do we build awareness (and to which audiences?) and create a vibrant, youthful, and borderline risqué brand in the more conservative, "nightlife-ends-early" city of Boston? How do we show we are a brand that wants to be playful and have fun?

- **High Street Place:** How do we relaunch a food hall in a neighborhood no longer full of office workers? If people no longer work in this neighborhood, how do we communicate with those who live nearby? How do we tell visitors or tourists to venture to the "financial district" for fun dining options? What experience should be there to make it worthwhile? How do we tell others beyond our radius that our offering is worth the trek? We are now trying to reach new audiences with different motivations for the same overarching experience—or is it the same?

- **The Kenmore:** Like the Smoke Shop example above (the need to help create traffic patterns and awareness in the local vicinity), how do we direct Red Sox fans to an affordable bar and restaurant just steps from Fenway Park and encourage them to walk one block east of the T (the transit system) rather than west? It's only one block in the other direction for a fun atmosphere with affordable cocktails and good food. How do we directly communicate with baseball fans to steer them toward this little gem of a hole-in-the-wall bar for their pre- or post-game social, even though the location is just a block or two away from the train line or "out of the way" for many fans?

- **The Verb:** This "rock and roll" themed hotel appeals to boomers and Gen X, but what about Millennials and Gen Zs? Aren't they current or prospective guests, too? After all, the Rock and Roll Hall of Fame in Cleveland isn't just about rock and roll anymore, is it? What should we do physically in the hotel, or digitally, as we position ourselves for a wider audience and a new generation of customers?

These brand repositioning initiatives highlight the essential role of adaptability and targeted communication in the hospitality industry and remind us to stay loyal to the brand while creating the experience for various guests. By thoughtfully understanding and addressing their unique market challenges, each brand successfully carved out distinct identities, resonated with new audiences, and reinforced their relevance, telling us that effective repositioning is critical to the sustained success and differentiation of the brand and the experience.

Product Re-Positioning for Customer Solution

Marketers must ensure messaging connects with customers or guests from their perspective, not ours. This conveys a shift from a product-centric approach to a customer-centric one. It's about reframing our strategies to align with the customer's needs and aspirations. Here are a few examples of brands that repositioned themselves from "product" to "customer solutions."

Amazon: Online Bookstore to "Everything Store"

It's impossible to talk about brand repositioning without mentioning Amazon. When Jeff Bezos launched the company in 1994, Amazon focused almost exclusively on selling books. The goal was to become the world's biggest bookstore, and for a while, that strategy worked. However, the demand for physical books declined, and Amazon knew it needed to adapt to meet the customer's needs, not just "sell the product."

Bezos and his team saw an opportunity to expand beyond books and transform Amazon into what it's now famously known as: the "Ultimate Online Marketplace." The company diversified its offerings, making it possible for consumers to purchase everything from electronics to home goods, all from a single platform. This repositioning wasn't just about adding more products; Amazon also ventured into different industries, with Zoox for autonomous vehicles and Amazon Web Services (AWS), which became a critical driver of the company's success in the tech world.

With an updated logo and a streamlined marketing approach, Amazon's repositioning paved the way for its evolution into the go-to online store for virtually every need. The company didn't stop there. Its success in e-commerce opened the door to even more innovation, leading to the development of products like the Amazon Echo smart speaker and advancements in AI technology.

Amazon's journey from online bookstore to a global retail and technology giant exemplifies how a brand can adapt, expand, and remain relevant through strategic repositioning. Today, Amazon is not just a store; it's an integral part of daily life for millions worldwide. It's a customer solution.

Play-Doh: Wallpaper Cleaner to Children's Creative Clay

Today, Play-Doh is a beloved household name, known for its vibrant modeling clay and various arts and crafts accessories. However, few people know that Play-Doh's origins had nothing to do with toys or creativity. When it first launched in the 1930s, the product was designed as a household cleaner, specifically to remove coal residue from wallpaper—a common problem at the time.

However, as homes transitioned to oil and gas heating in the 1950s, the need for such a product drastically declined, and Play-Doh's business was in trouble. Then came an unexpected discovery. A teacher in Cincinnati was using the clay cleaner in her classroom for arts and crafts projects with children, which sparked an idea for a complete rebranding.

Play-Doh shifted its focus, creating colorful, non-toxic clay specifically for kids. This repositioning proved to be a brilliant move, transforming Play-Doh from a fading cleaning product into a creative tool for children's play and education. By 1991, Hasbro saw its potential and acquired the brand. Since then, Play-Doh has sold over two billion jars, securing its place in homes and classrooms around the world. What began as a practical household cleaner became one of the most popular and enduring toys of all time and a testament to the power of smart repositioning and adaptability.

Netflix: From DVD Rental Service to Streaming and Movie Production Powerhouse

In the late 1990s, Netflix began as a DVD rental service, offering a convenient alternative to traditional video stores. Customers could order DVDs online and have them mailed directly to their homes, eliminating late fees and the hassle of returning movies. While this innovative model gained traction, the landscape of entertainment was rapidly changing.

As the popularity of streaming technology grew, Netflix recognized a pivotal opportunity to transform its business. Rather than sticking to its original model, the company made a bold move in 2007 by launching its streaming service. This shift allowed subscribers to instantly access a vast library of movies and TV shows from the comfort of their homes, marking a significant pivot in how people consumed media.

However, Netflix didn't stop there. Recognizing the power of original content, the company began investing in producing its own films and series, starting with hits like *House of Cards* and *Orange Is the New Black*. This strategy differentiated Netflix from other streaming services and positioned it as a formidable player in the entertainment industry.

Today, Netflix is synonymous with streaming, with over 300 million subscribers worldwide (as of May 2025) and a robust catalog of original programming that includes award-winning films and series. The transformation from a DVD rental company to a leading streaming and production powerhouse exemplifies how adaptability and vision can redefine a brand and reshape an entire industry.

Starbucks: Your Third Place to a Quality Cup of Coffee

Howard Schultz transformed the coffee experience by turning Starbucks into what he called the "third place"—a comfortable spot outside of home and work where people could gather. This concept played a key role in Starbucks' early success, helping it grow into a global enterprise where customers could socialize or unwind with a cup of coffee.

However, by 2008, the rapid expansion of Starbucks led to problems. The brand's quality of service couldn't keep up with its increasing number of locations, and its focus had become diluted. In its attempt to be more than just a coffeehouse, Starbucks began offering non-coffee products, like music, which pulled attention away from its core identity. Then, as consumers turned to less expensive alternatives such as McDonald's, Starbucks was forced to close over 900 stores as American budgets tightened.

These challenges prompted a major repositioning. Starbucks needed to remind the world of what it stood for, and that's exactly what they did. With the launch of their largest-ever marketing campaign, "coffee value and values," the company focused on reaffirming the quality of their product and why it was worth the extra cost. The campaign used bold, memorable slogans like "Beware a cheaper cup of coffee. It comes with a price," and "Starbucks or nothing. Because compromise leaves a really bad aftertaste." Starbucks even promised to remake a customer's coffee if it wasn't perfect, emphasizing their commitment to delivering an exceptional product.

The repositioning worked. By 2014, Starbucks had bounced back, reporting a record $16 billion in annual revenue. This transformation serves as one of the strongest examples of a brand returning to its roots, reaffirming that its identity wasn't about being a catch-all third place but about delivering a high-quality cup of coffee. In simplifying and clarifying its message, Starbucks managed to recover and thrive.

Airbnb: Spare Room Rental to Hospitality Revolution

Airbnb began in 2008 as a simple idea: Founders Brian Chesky, Joe Gebbia, and Nathan Blecharczyk wanted to help travelers find affordable places to stay. They started by renting out air mattresses in their San Francisco apartment during a design conference, essentially providing a spare room for guests. This novel approach quickly gained traction, but the founders recognized the potential for something much larger.

As the travel landscape evolved, so did Airbnb. The company repositioned itself from a platform for renting spare rooms to a comprehensive hospitality service that caters to diverse traveler needs. They expanded their offerings to include entire homes; unique accommodations, such as treehouses and castles; and even experiences hosted by locals, allowing guests to immerse themselves in the culture of their destination.

Airbnb's marketing strategy emphasized the idea of "Belong Anywhere," highlighting the personal connection between hosts and guests. This messaging resonated with consumers seeking authentic travel experiences that traditional hotels couldn't provide. The platform also introduced measures to enhance trust and safety, such as host and guest reviews, secure payments, and customer support.

Airbnb has transformed the way people think about travel and accommodation, becoming a global leader in the hospitality industry. With millions of listings in over 200 countries, Airbnb's evolution reflects a successful repositioning that meets the changing preferences of modern travelers, prioritizing community, authenticity, and unique experiences.

These examples show that a clear brand identity backed by purposeful evolution can elevate a company from a "product provider" to an integral part of customers' lives. By consistently delivering on their why and curating brand-aligned experiences, Amazon, Play-Doh, Netflix, Starbucks, and Airbnb have proven that staying true to a core promise while adapting to consumer needs is the key to enduring success. They understand their brand and the experience delivered. They remained relevant.

Ultimately, a brand is a promise, and the experience is how customers feel that promise come to life. By integrating consistent branding, personalizing interactions, and ensuring alignment at every touchpoint, marketers create not just a product or service but a meaningful connection that keeps customers returning time and again.

Marketing Mantras

1. **Understand the Importance of Branding:**
   Recognize that branding is essential for effective marketing. It establishes a business's identity, values, and promise, which shape and guide marketing strategies. Marketing efforts cannot begin without a clear understanding of the product, service, and brand experience.

2. **Brand Value, Not Just Colors and Logos:**
   A brand is more than just colors and logos; it's the value proposition and the experience customers have with the product at every interaction

point. It involves the emotional connection consumers have with the company. Brand identity includes elements like mission, vision, values, and personality. These elements influence how marketing messages are crafted and delivered.

3. **Maintain Consistency in Branding:**

   Consistency in branding across all marketing channels is crucial. This includes consistency in look, voice, tone, and promise, which helps build a reliable and trustworthy brand.

4. **Develop a Clear Brand Strategy:**

   A clear brand strategy forms a framework for marketing campaigns, helping marketers understand how to position products or services in the market and differentiate them from competitors.

5. **Build Relationships at Every Touchpoint:**

   Effective branding builds relationships at every touchpoint, whether digital, physical, or through word-of-mouth. Each touchpoint can enhance or harm the brand, making delivering appropriate and meaningful interactions essential. These micro-moments evoke emotion and are critical to customer connection.

6. **Learn From Successful Brands:**

   Successful brands like Apple, Starbucks, and Disney convey distinct values and maintain authenticity while evolving to remain relevant and meaningful to their audiences. Brands should be durable, evolvable, and the go-to solution for customers.

7. **Balance Marketing Promises:**

   Marketers must balance promises in their messaging to ensure they do not overpromise and underdeliver or underpromise and lose potential customers. Creating memorable experiences and marketing them effectively is crucial.

8. **Shift to Customer-Centric Strategies:**

   Marketing strategies should shift from product-centric to customer-centric, focusing on the customer's needs and desires. This involves researching, listening to customers, and personalizing experiences to build strong emotional connections.

9. **Embrace Personalization in Marketing:**

   In today's connected world, consumers seek personalized experiences. Marketers must craft messages and experiences that resonate with individuals, anticipating their needs and delighting them in unexpected ways. This personalization helps build emotional bonds with customers.

Combine Brand Identity with Memorable Experiences: Brand identity and memorable experiences lead to marketing success. Marketers can achieve sustained growth and customer loyalty by ensuring that every interaction reinforces the brand's core values and creates lasting impressions.

As we've explored, a robust and consistent brand forms the foundation and throughline of effective marketing. With a solid brand in place, the next natural step is to explore how we can leverage this strong foundation to expand our reach and offerings. In the upcoming chapter on brand extensions, we understand how broadening a brand's impact by introducing new products or services or entering new markets (while maintaining the integrity and essence of the original brand) can unlock new opportunities to drive continued success.

Mindset in Motion

Consider your brand or the brands you admire. Reflect on how they create memorable experiences for their customers. Document specific examples of how these brands embody authenticity and deliver on their promises. Then, think about your target audience: What emotional connections can you foster through personalized experiences? Identify three micro-moments in your customer journey where you can enhance engagement and strengthen brand loyalty. This exercise will help you recognize the integral relationship between brand and experience, guiding you to create deeper connections with your customers.

4

Brand Extensions and Positioning for Growth

Thinking like a marketer means understanding how brand extensions have become a pivotal strategy for businesses aiming to diversify and grow. By leveraging the equity of an established brand, companies can seamlessly enter new product categories or industries, capitalizing on the trust and loyalty they've built over time. This demands a delicate balance of maintaining the core brand promise while ensuring an appropriate fit with the new vertical to avoid brand dilution or consumer confusion.

What Makes a Brand Successful?

Understanding Brand Extensions

A marketing mindset will recognize that brand extensions offer a powerful way to leverage a strong value proposition into new, related opportunities that drive growth and profitability. Now, let's explore a variety of hospitality-focused case studies to understand how brands successfully apply their core promise to other verticals, creating new avenues for innovation and customer engagement.

Lodging Brand Examples

Brand extensions offer significant financial advantages and allow established hospitality brands to diversify their offerings and tap into new revenue streams. According to Statista, the global vacation ownership market was valued at approximately $12 billion in 2020, with Hilton and Marriott significantly contributing through their brand extensions (Hilton Grand Vacations and Marriott Vacation Club). These strategic extensions have enabled the hotel companies to diversify their offerings, create additional revenue streams, and reinforce their market positions.

In reverse scenarios, notable brands are extending into the hospitality landscape. Luxury goods brands are increasingly expanding into the hospitality sector, leveraging their established prestige and brand equity to create exclusive hotel and resort experiences. This strategic extension allows brands like Louis Vuitton and Armani to offer immersive environments reflecting their unique aesthetic and values, deepening customer engagement and diversifying revenue streams. More on that in a moment.

When extending a brand into new verticals, it's crucial to retain the essence of the brand promise—the core values, quality, and emotional connection customers associate with the brand. The new product or service should naturally align with these attributes to ensure coherence and authenticity. Additionally, the new vertical should be a logical fit for the brand, meaning it complements the brand's existing image and customer base, rather than diluting or confusing the brand identity.

Several notable examples in the lodging and restaurant worlds illustrate successful brand extensions. For instance, some restaurants have ventured into retail by offering their culinary products in supermarkets. TGI Fridays, for example, extended its family-friendly, casual dining offering of American food and drink in brick-and-mortar restaurants around the United States into frozen food products available in grocery stores. This extension allows customers to enjoy TGI Fridays at home, maintaining the brand's promise of fun dining experiences while fitting seamlessly into the retail food sector.

Another compelling example is the Paris-based brand LVMH (Moët Hennessy Louis Vuitton), a multi-national holding company and conglomerate specializing in luxury. LVMH controls nearly sixty subsidiaries that manage seventy-five luxury brands, including Tiffany, Dior, Fendi, Givenchy, Celine, Sephora, TAG Heuer, and Bulgari. LVMH extended into the lodging business with its Cheval Blanc and Belmond hotel brands. By entering the luxury hospitality market, LVMH has maintained its promise of exclusivity, sophistication, and high-end experiences. This brand extension fits well with LVMH's existing image, offering their clientele luxurious stays and mirroring the elegance and refinement of their fashion and lifestyle products.

Belmond and Cheval Blanc offer LVMH opportunities to broaden its luxury offerings, leveraging existing brand equity to enter and excel in the hospitality sector. When thoughtfully executed, these examples show how brand extensions can enhance brand equity, reach new customer segments, and create additional revenue streams.

A few other examples of brand extensions in hospitality are likely very familiar:

1. **Ritz-Carlton:**

   - **Retail Products:** The Ritz-Carlton has extended its luxury brand into retail with products such as The Ritz-Carlton Reserve Fragrance Collection, which captures the essence of their most iconic destinations in a line of high-end scents. (https://www. ritzcarltonshops.com/)

- **Residences:** Luxury residences bring the Ritz-Carlton hospitality experience into private homes, allowing customers to enjoy the brand's standards of service and luxury in their everyday lives. (https://www.ritzcarlton. com/en/residences/)

2. **Hilton:**

- **Hilton Home Collection:** Hilton offers a home collection line featuring their signature bedding, pillows, and other in-room products. This allows guests to recreate the Hilton experience in their homes. (https://www.hiltontohome.com/)
- **Timeshares:** Through Hilton Grand Vacations, Hilton provides timeshare opportunities, extending the Hilton hospitality experience to vacation ownership and promoting a consistent brand experience for frequent travelers.

3. **Marriott:**

- **Marriott Bonvoy Boutiques:** Marriott offers customers the ability to purchase the beds, linens, towels, and even art from their favorite Marriott brands through the Marriott

Bonvoy Boutiques online store. (https://www.boutiques.marriottbonvoy.com/)

- **Vacation Club:** Marriott Vacation Club allows members to own timeshares in various locations, extending the hotel experience to vacation properties worldwide. (https://www.hiltongrandvacations.com/)

Restaurants Examples

1. **Nobu:**

   - **Hotels:** Nobu, originally a high-end Japanese restaurant, has extended its brand into the hotel industry with Nobu Hotels. These properties blend luxurious accommodations with Nobu's signature culinary excellence, offering a cohesive brand experience. (https://www.nobuhotels.com/)

   - **Cookbooks and Products:** Nobu also offers cookbooks and specialty food products, allowing fans to recreate the Nobu experience at home. (https://www.noburestaurants.com/home/nobu-at-home-2)

2. **Starbucks:**

   - **Consumer Products:** Starbucks has extended its brand into consumer-packaged goods, offering products like Starbucks coffee beans, ready-to-drink beverages, and K-Cups available in grocery stores worldwide.

- **Teavana:** By acquiring and promoting the Teavana brand, Starbucks expanded into the premium tea market, providing a complementary product line to their core coffee offerings.

3. **Shake Shack:**

- **Retail Food Products:** Shake Shack has introduced products such as ShackSauce and Shake Shack-branded beef patties in supermarkets, allowing customers to enjoy some of their favorite menu items at home.
- **Cookbook:** The Shake Shack cookbook shares recipes and insights from the restaurant, helping fans replicate the experience in their own kitchens. (https://www.goodreads.com/book/show/33517094-shake-shack)

Classroom Cases

In our classes over the years, we have been posed with marketing challenges and assignments pertaining to brand extensions. And they are fun to study and execute. For example:

Boulangerie Blend: Integrating a Bakery with a Local French Dining Experience: Rochambeau is a brasserie in Boston's Back Bay owned by the locally famed Lyons Group. As experts in concept development, design, construction, and marketing, the Lyons Group was originally established as an entertainment company focused on dance clubs and producing over 300 live shows annually. In the 1990s, it expanded into the world of restaurants and today oversees the creative offerings of "an array of venues in six states, encompassing free-standing establishments, hotel collaborations and casino ventures." Rochambeau is its French restaurant with a strong following. Now it was time for our students to devise the marketing plan for the bakery located on the street level at the entrance of the restaurant.

How can we position this bakery-café as a "go-to" for the office workers and residents of the Prudential Center and encourage coffee, pastry, or sandwich menus for breakfast or lunch? How do we suggest that people who live in the area, people who work there, and those who visit the area no longer head to Starbucks or (Massachusetts-based) Dunkin'? This is a brave brand extension in the challenging, competitive space of morning bakery cafés and coffee places. Was the Rochambeau value proposition strong enough to lure locals to come to its sister café and order a morning or lunchtime coffee?

Retail Rendezvous: Linking Hotel and Local Shop: In 2021, the Boston Harbor Hotel (BHH) on the waterfront opened its boutique, a partnership with the South End's eclectic art and home shop, Modern Relik. The store is no longer part of the hotel today, but at the time, the challenge was two-fold: First, how does the luxury hotel connect with new customers as it opens this fine retail shop offering linens, furniture, and décor found in the hotel rooms? How can it market to fans of the upscale home goods store? Second, how do they name the store, so it resonates in customers' minds, connecting the classic lodging with the contemporary home décor retailer? The students disagreed with the impending name of the store—HOME at Rowes Wharf. To convey the brand extension and familiar experience, the students recommended "Modern Relik@the Boston Harbor Hotel." We were concerned the name "HOME" could also inadvertently imply "residences" at Rowes Wharf (condos), and our interviews implied awareness of Rowes Wharf wasn't as strong as awareness for the hotel itself.

These brand extensions, along with the earlier industry examples, illustrate the importance of strategic alignment and differentiation. By thoughtfully leveraging existing brand strengths and addressing unique market challenges, can we identify distinct and appealing offerings resonating with new target audiences while reinforcing the core brand identity? That's the challenge.

From Packages to Personalized Experiences: Elevating Brand Extensions

"Packages?" No.

"Experiences?" Yes!

As a post-pandemic world has demonstrated, people are craving the opportunity to make memories and indulge in once-in-a-lifetime dreams. We are living in an "experience-driven" society, and part of our marketing effort needs to elevate our brands to deliver meaningful aspects of these experiences. I encourage our students to stop calling hotel packages, "packages." It sounds "commodity-like" and impersonal. But if we create "experiences" tailored and personalized for meaningful events or memories, we will have success. I'd rather purchase a hotel's Valentine's Experience, which will be robust with elements I find meaningful, rather than a Valentine's Package when every hotel offers the same set of elements to every guest. This means there is nothing particularly special just for me. This shift in terminology emphasizes the curated, personalized nature of what we offer, highlighting the transformative potential of a stay with us. By focusing on experiences, we cater to the growing demand for meaningful and impactful moments, setting ourselves apart in a competitive space.

When our class worked with the Copley Plaza Hotel and the Langham Hotel (at different times and with differing challenges), the students encouraged the sales and marketing directors to create "experiences" rather than posting a website tab called "packages." The experiences enabled guests and web visitors to ask for customized changes, which can generate revenue for the hotels. In this manner, the hotel comes through as a trusted place for guests to have the experience they wanted.

This strategic shift, with the word experiences, emphasizes value beyond the tangible elements. Additionally, by calling them experiences, businesses align their offerings with these expectations, attracting customers who prioritize meaningful interactions over simple transactions.

Experiences are often perceived as higher quality, can justify premium pricing, and create a sense of exclusivity that distinguishes the brand from competitors. Experiences evoke emotions, and emotional connections are powerful drivers of customer loyalty and advocacy.

The concept of an experience lends itself well to storytelling, a critical component of effective marketing. It allows businesses to craft narratives around their offerings, engaging customers and leading to more effective marketing campaigns.

And once again, the "P" word—personalization. Experiences can be more easily tailored to individual preferences and needs, enhancing personalization and improving satisfaction and loyalty.

Partnership Potentials: Enhancing Brand Positioning and Visibility

Brand partnerships are highly beneficial for several reasons. First, they allow businesses to leverage the credibility and customer base of another established brand, which can lead to increased brand awareness and trust.

By associating with a reputable partner, companies can enhance their brand image and reach a wider audience more effectively than they could on their own. Additionally, partnerships enable cost-sharing for marketing campaigns, making it more economical to execute large-scale promotional activities. This combination also fosters innovation because combining resources and expertise from different entities leads to the creation of unique products or services that would not have developed independently.

Identifying brands from other industries for partnerships can significantly expand a company's marketing reach. For example, a tech company partnering with a fashion line can tap into the fashion industry's customer base, creating opportunities for unique marketing initiatives for the audiences of both brands. This approach also introduces new dimensions to the brand's identity, making it more versatile and appealing. By exploring synergies with brands in different sectors, companies can innovate and create compelling value propositions to stand out in a cluttered marketplace.

Students' Recommendation: Culinary Couture: A French Restaurant x Fashion Line Pop-Up

In the fall of 2018, a wonderful team of students worked with one of Boston's legendary restaurants, French-Mediterranean dining destination, Mistral. Chef and owner Jamie Mammano opened the restaurant in

1997 and built it "inspired by the breezy essence of the French Riviera, showcasing the freshest seasonal ingredients" (mistralbistro.com). A "Provencal charm" ambiance features "hand-selected French ceramics and sweeping arched windows exuding warmth and sophistication." The students creatively thought of adding "pop-up" restaurants for more physical visibility (based on extensive market research) and recommended a national partnership with clothing brand Club Monaco. The students assessed the brand and compared the values, finding similarities and alignment with those of Mistral.

The team wanted to "take the pop-up experience one step further," especially since it's an effective tool to engage with new customers locally and nationally. At the time, Club Monaco was a subsidiary of Ralph Lauren Corporation and was an upscale, young, and vibrant brand. Conceptually, Club Monaco represented "taking the trusted classics and revitalizing them for current market trends." Therefore, Mistral perfectly aligned with Club Monaco from a brand message perspective since both were lifestyle brands. Both companies, at the time of these recommendations, offered aspirational products that the average consumer could consume frequently. While this partnership was merely a student team recommendation, it demonstrates the critical and strategic thinking involved in the research.

By focusing on shared values and complementary strengths, brands can create synergies that drive mutual growth and success. Brand partnerships that transcend industries can offer a variety of benefits, including:

1. **Expanded Reach and Enhanced Credibility:**
   Collaborating with brands from different industries allows partners to access new customer bases, increasing visibility and market share. Partnering with a well-regarded brand lends credibility and trustworthiness to newer or less-established brands, strengthening their reputation.

2. **Innovative Offerings and Shared Resources:**
   Combining expertise from diverse sectors fosters the creation of unique products or services that would be unattainable within a single industry. Brands can share marketing budgets, distribution channels, and specialized knowledge, reducing costs and enhancing operational efficiency.

3. **Cross-Promotion and Increased Engagement:**
   Leveraging each other's marketing channels, such as social media, email lists, and events, enables effective promotion of joint initiatives or products. Creative collaborations generate buzz and excitement among consumers, fostering stronger emotional connections and higher engagement levels.

4. **Competitive Advantage and Long-Term Growth:**
   Unique partnerships differentiate brands from their competitors, offering distinctive market

positions that appeal to consumers. Successful collaborations can evolve into long-term relationships, driving continuous innovation and mutual growth.

5. **Social Impact and Learning Opportunities:**

Brand partnerships can be utilized to promote social causes, enhancing both brands' reputations while positively impacting communities. Brands gain valuable insights by learning from each other's strengths and weaknesses, informing their strategies and operations for future success.

Here are a few interesting examples of large-scale brand collaborations:

1. **Extreme Synergy: GoPro x Red Bull:**

In May 2016, a groundbreaking collaboration was announced that would reshape the way we experience adventure and extreme sports. GoPro, the innovative company known for its cutting-edge cameras, joined forces with Red Bull, a global leader in energy drinks and extreme sports media. This multi-year partnership was built on a shared vision: to inspire individuals to live life to the fullest and capture every exhilarating moment along the way.

At the heart of this alliance, GoPro became Red Bull's exclusive provider of "point-of-view" imaging technology. This meant that Red Bull's extensive media productions and events—over

1,800 happening in over 100 countries—would be captured with GoPro's revolutionary cameras. The partnership allowed for a harmonious blend of content production, distribution, and cross-promotion, enhancing both brands' reach and impact.

2. **Tech Meets Fitness: Apple x Nike:**

   One of the most innovative cross-brand collaborations in recent memory is the partnership between Apple and Nike. This alliance brought together Nike's deep understanding of sports and fitness with Apple's unparalleled expertise in technology, resulting in the creation of the Nike+ iPod. This groundbreaking product allowed athletes and fitness enthusiasts to integrate music with their workouts seamlessly and efficiently. With the Nike+ sensor placed in shoes and synced to the iPod, users could track their performance while listening to their favorite songs, creating a personalized and motivating experience. This partnership demonstrated the power of blending two distinct industries—sports and technology—and marked a shift in how consumers engaged with both brands, making fitness more interactive and enjoyable.

3. **Fashion Bites: Warby Parker x Arby's:**

   In 2018, a most unexpected collaboration was announced: All eyes (pun intended) were on Warby's, and its unusual partnership with the sandwich chain Arby's. This partnership shook up the fast-fashion and fast-food landscapes with a limited-edition collection that included branded tees, baseball caps, pool slides, tote bags, raw beef-patterned glasses, and sandwich-themed microfiber cloths. (This launched on April Fool's Day.)

For those in New York, select Warby's locations offered a unique treat: the Onion Ring Monocle, a playful fusion of food and fashion. This quirky accessory company invited customers to engage with the brands in a fun and memorable way.

Arby's and Warby Parker donated proceeds to nonprofit organizations to celebrate their partnership. They supported VisionSpring, which works to make affordable eyeglasses accessible for all, ensuring everyone has the tools to lead a productive life, and No Kid Hungry, a national campaign focused on ending childhood hunger. Together, these brands made a fashion statement and championed meaningful causes.

By combining their unique strengths and expertise, these brands successfully created innovative products, expanded their audience reach, and enhanced customer engagement, thanks to effective cross-industry collaborations.

Leveraging Strong Brand Equity for Successful Extensions

Former student and teaching assistant Kim Kibler and I also recently chatted about *brand identity* versus *brand reputation*. In recapping the conversation, I'd tell you brand identity is what you create; brand reputation is what you earn. In today's world, where options are abundant, reputation is everything. Remember, perception is someone's reality, and it's the reputation you build that determines whether your brand stands out or fades into the noise.

From Coffee to Cork: Leveraging Brand Excellence to Enter the Wine Market

Brand extensions succeed when they build upon the reputation and trust a brand has already established in its core offering. Take, for example, George Howell Wines.

Classroom Case in Point: George Howell is a pioneering figure in the coffee industry, widely recognized for creating the iconic Frappuccino. After selling the rights to Starbucks, which held exclusive use of the term for two decades, Howell shifted his focus back to his passion: elevating the art and science of coffee. When the rights reverted to him, he returned to the scene with a renewed mission, opening coffee shops with retail stores in the Boston area. Through his brand, George Howell Coffee, he has continued to champion quality, sustainability, and innovation, solidifying his reputation as a leader and visionary in specialty coffee.

My students were tasked by George Howell Coffee COO Rebecca Fitzgerald to help market the new wine offerings in Boston's Downtown Crossing location. George Howell built his name and reputation by curating exceptional coffees, earning the trust of consumers who associate his brand with quality and expertise. This strong foundation made it possible to extend the brand into wines, leveraging the same principles of thoughtful selection and reliability. Customers who value the brand's discernment in one category are more likely to trust its choices in a related category, demonstrating how a well-regarded reputation can be the cornerstone for successful diversification.

Employer Branding as a Brand Extension

Employer branding is now as crucial to brand extension as any product or service offered. As shared earlier, authentic employee testimonials and a strong workplace culture can be the difference between struggling to fill positions and building a thriving, engaged workforce. Today, employer branding has emerged as a vital component of brand extension strategies. It involves promoting the company as a desirable place to work, attracting top talent, and fostering a positive internal culture. This form of brand extension enhances the company's reputation and ensures that employees embody the brand's values and promise.

The shifting employment landscape has made it more challenging to attract talent. That is why employers must now pay special attention to how they present themselves to potential new hires, actively marketing their products and services as well as their culture, values, and employee experience.

In industries centered around service, nothing speaks louder than the voices of satisfied team members. Testimonials and peer endorsements resonate more strongly than traditional promotional messages when it comes to recruitment. Companies must highlight authentic stories and experiences from their current employees—what they love about their jobs, how they feel supported and appreciated, and how they find meaningful connections with customers.

A prime example comes from the innovative ways employers are leveraging social media. As my former teaching assistant Elise Borkan Mackin, who now works in a communications role at a prestigious country club, notes, short-form TikTok videos have proven highly effective in capturing attention and humanizing the workplace. These quick, visually engaging snippets showcase employees' genuine enthusiasm for their day-to-day tasks and cultivate a sense of community and camaraderie, which in turn "appeals to job seekers looking for a positive work environment."

The earlier Mercure app example of personalized connection with guests can transform into an employer branding USP (unique selling proposition). Mercure by AccorHotels utilized the Facebook Messenger chatbot, Mercure Bot, to engage with both guests and potential employees. Mercure Bot reinforced the brand's commitment to innovation and customer satisfaction by providing personalized recommendations and streamlined customer interactions. This enhanced the guest experience and showcased AccorHotels as a forward-thinking employer, thereby creating potential for attracting tech-savvy talent interested in working with cutting-edge technologies.

Through these varying examples, from TGI Fridays' retail ventures to LVMH's luxury hospitality acquisitions, we see that extensions can significantly enhance brand equity, reach new customer segments, and create additional revenue streams. As digital advancements and consumer preferences continue to shift and evolve, the ability to adapt and innovate through thoughtful brand extensions will remain a critical success factor for businesses.

Just as a well-executed brand extension can elevate a business, the name of a brand or product itself serves as a powerful extension of the brand's identity. The right name sets the tone for consumer perception and plays a pivotal role in the success or failure of a brand's offerings. In the hospitality industry, we've seen firsthand how a poorly chosen name can adversely impact a brand's reputation, customer perception, and overall market success.

What's In a Name?

The Importance of a Name for a Brand and Extensions

Why is the name of a business so critical, and why can it impact the marketing? How can a name, which could be confusing or easily forgettable, adversely impact the experience?

The importance of a product or service having the right name cannot be overstated. A well-chosen name can significantly impact marketing efforts, brand recognition, and overall success. First impressions matter. The name is the first point of contact between the product or service and the consumer. A strong, memorable name can create an immediate positive impression and facilitate quick recognition. A catchy or intriguing name can pique curiosity and encourage potential customers to learn more about the product or service. The name can convey elements of the brand's story, values, and personality, helping build a deeper connection with the target audience.

A name that is easy to pronounce, spell, and remember enhances marketing efforts across various channels, making it easier for consumers to recall and refer to the product or service. As shared below, a well-chosen name can also improve search engine optimization (SEO) and social media presence, making it easier for potential customers to find the product or service online.

Names that evoke positive emotions or associations can enhance the overall appeal of the product or service. It can create a sense of trust, excitement, or reliability in the minds of consumers. Certain names can trigger psychological responses, helping convey the brand's desired image or message. For example, a luxury brand might choose a sophisticated name to evoke a sense of elegance and exclusivity.

Selecting a name that is legally available and can be trademarked is essential to protect the brand and avoid legal disputes. Always remember that having an available domain name is crucial for establishing an online presence. If the product or service is marketed globally, the name must be appropriate and well-received across different cultures and languages. Missteps in this area can lead to negative perceptions and reduced market acceptance.

So, who has an effective name? Apple. The name is simple, easy to remember, and stands out in the tech industry. This is great for simplicity and recall. It also conveys a sense of approachability and innovation.

An effective name that communicates its core service is Airbnb. It is easy to pronounce and projects hospitality and travel.

Nike is symbolic and strong. Named after the Greek goddess of victory, the name Nike commands strength, performance, and triumph, aligning perfectly with the brand's athletic focus.

Entrepreneurs take note: the name of your product can make or break its success.

Identity Reimagined: The Healthcare System's Renaming Journey: In class, we study the rebranding of the North Shore LIJ hospitals on Long Island and discuss at length the impact of its branding as a healthcare system, and name, Northwell Health. (The Northwell name was announced in the fall of 2015 and officially launched in January 2016.)

The name and brand "Northwell" resulted from years of contemplation, four outside consulting agencies, and an initial list of 5,000 names whittled down over time to the final few. I applaud the name in our class discussion for various reasons: It combines geographic relevance, positive connotations, an upward direction, simplicity, memorability, and a strong brand promise. It conveys professionalism, trust, and a commitment to overall wellness, making it a strong and resonant choice for a healthcare system. The name helps the organization stand out while fostering a sense of community and assurance among patients.

New Names: Transforming Hotel Identities with Resulting Confusion: In my career, I had the responsibility of marketing the renaming of the Sheraton Centre

Hotel and the Sheraton City Squire Hotel (which were across the street from one another) to the Sheraton New York Hotel and Towers and the Sheraton Manhattan. Well, how can that not possibly be confusing? One hotel was literally called "New York," and the other "Manhattan." (Both hotels have slightly different names today.)

Marketing the renaming of the two behemoth properties presented a unique challenge. With both hotels established as prominent in a bustling city, the task was not just about changing names; it was about creating a clear distinction between the two entities that could easily blend into a single identity in the minds of customers, taxi drivers, travel agents, and more. The similarities in the names, combined with the proximity of the hotels, meant that we had to be deliberate and strategic in our communications. Every piece of marketing material needed to reinforce the individuality of each hotel and highlight their distinct features and offerings.

This wasn't easy as both hotels appealed to a similar market mix, were priced competitively with one another, and enabled guests to use the amenities at the other hotel. One important difference was that the Sheraton Manhattan was one of a few hotels featuring an indoor swimming pool. The Sheraton New York offered premium-level room accommodations and the excitement of a large cosmopolitan hotel.

Clear communication was paramount. We developed campaigns that educated the public about the new names and provided meeting planners, travel agents, corporate planners, and, yes, taxi drivers with easily digestible information to avoid any confusion when directing guests. The messaging needed to resonate with our target audiences, ensuring each hotel stood out while still embodying the quality and service synonymous with the renovated and repositioned Sheraton brand. The timing of these renamings is important. This was before the onset of Google Search, which presents a whole other set of considerations when marketing your name.

Clear Choices: Renaming Restaurants for Customer Clarity: Similarly, let's take a look at Outlook and Lookout. Yes, I said this correctly. Lookout and Outlook were two different restaurants at the Envoy Hotel in the Seaport neighborhood of Boston. We brought in my dear friends Joe Mellia, former general manager of the hotel, Food Network star chef Tatiana Rosana, and the hotel's food and beverage director, Josh Glover, who explained to us that the hotel needed help marketing its lobby-level three-meal café restaurant, called Outlook. "Lookout" is the name of the hotel's rooftop bar area with igloos for sitting and shmoozing, fun cocktails, and fantastic views of Boston Harbor. The restaurants were named by the ownership of the hotel because it was fun to have a lobby-level "Outlook" and a rooftop "Lookout." Both were named with good intentions.

However, as fun as it was intended to be, it didn't work. The names caused irritation and confusion. When the students analyzed online reputation management, reviewing comments online in Yelp, Google, and other sites, they quickly noticed a pattern: Too many guests continually confused the names of the restaurants. When the student team dug further and conducted a Google search for Outlook, even Google was confused because some of the Outlook information was inadvertently put into the wrong restaurant listings. Names are important. And today, names need to be "Google-able." Confusion because of poor names can trigger a negative experience. The students had to build enough nerve to recommend that Joe consider changing the restaurant's name. It's very hard to tell someone to change their "baby's" name, especially when named by the owner. As soon as the students uttered the words, "We recommend an immediate name change," Josh immediately threw his arms in the air and shouted, "Yes!"

We were so relieved. Josh admitted he was hoping the students would say this to prove what he already knew. Sure enough, since then, the restaurant has been re-imagined, and it's now called Para Maria with a menu as an homage to Chef Tatiana's Cuban heritage.

Name Makeover: Transforming an Unappealing Moniker: In the Fall 2021 semester, we worked with the team developing the start-up app intended to share a calendar of local Boston events. It was to be a seamless platform to find things to do—events, festivals, after-hours museum parties, newly-opened restaurants and bars, and more. The concept was intriguing and garnered great investor and consumer focus group interest. But the name? I can't share it here due to the NDAs our students signed. However, I will say that the student team immediately challenged the name, concerned it projected something delicious or, frankly, something completely inappropriate. The app launched and hired one of the student team members part-time after graduation. The developers ultimately changed the name to something a bit easier to roll off the tongue and less cutesy for what the app is designed to deliver.

Marketing Mantras

1. **Leverage Existing Brand Equity:**
   Brand extension involves utilizing an existing brand's equity to enter new product categories or industries. By capitalizing on your established reputation, trust, and customer loyalty, you can reduce the risks and costs associated with launching new products.

2. **Maintain Core Brand Promise:**
   Successful brand extensions must retain the core brand promise and ensure the new vertical aligns with the brand's values, quality, and emotional connection. This maintains coherence and authenticity, ensuring the extension feels like a natural progression of the brand.

3. **Shift from Packages to Experiences:**

   Transitioning terminology from "packages" to "experiences" emphasizes your offerings' curated, personalized nature. This caters to the growing demand for meaningful and impactful moments, setting your brand apart in a competitive space.

4. **Utilize Brand Partnerships:**

   Brand partnerships allow businesses to leverage another established brand's credibility and customer base. This expands market reach and creates unique, innovative products or services by bridging both brands' audiences.

5. **Choose Memorable Names:**

   A well-chosen name significantly impacts marketing, brand recognition, and overall success. It should be memorable, convey the brand's story, values, and personality, and be easy to pronounce, spell, and remember, thereby enhancing marketing efforts and consumer recall.

6. **Invest in Employer Branding:**

   Employer branding is now as crucial to brand extension as any product or service you offer. Authentic employee testimonials and a strong workplace culture can be the difference between struggling to fill positions and building a thriving, engaged workforce.

7. **Strategize New Revenue Streams:**

   Continuously brainstorm and strategize new revenue streams, partnerships, or opportunities to strengthen your brand value. Innovative ideas in these areas can lead to sustainable growth and reinforce your brand's market position.

With a strategy for brand extensions in place, the next critical step is to define where we want our brand to go. Understanding our ultimate objectives allows us to set clear expectations and develop actionable plans to achieve them. In "Start with the End Goals," we delve into the importance of establishing clear objectives, setting realistic expectations, and determining the strategic steps necessary to turn our vision into reality.

Mindset in Motion

Reflect on a brand extension you've encountered, either positively or negatively. What factors contributed to its success or failure? Identify a brand you're familiar with and brainstorm potential extensions that align with its core identity. Consider how these extensions can enhance customer experiences and leverage existing brand equity. Then, think about the importance of naming in this process: What would be key considerations when choosing a name for a new extension? Write down your thoughts on how to ensure that brand extensions feel authentic and resonate with customers, keeping in mind the balance between innovation and the brand's established identity.

5

Start with the End Goals

When strategically marketing, starting with the end in mind ensures clarity, focus, and measurable success. Whether launching a new campaign or extending a brand, defining clear goals and aligning metrics with those goals is critical. Marketers can use this "back-planning" approach to create more impactful strategies.

As my friend Pete Rosenblum, president of NYC-based marketing, publicity, and advertising agency MAP360Co reiterates to my students when he guest lectures, "Start by identifying what the goals are, and know your budget to get there."

Start with Clarity

Before diving into campaign planning, ask yourself: "What does success truly look like for this effort?" This initial clarity shapes every decision ahead, from creative direction to budget allocation. In the hospitality industry, success isn't one-size-fits-all. For some campaigns, it might mean heightened brand awareness among luxury travelers. For others, it's all about increasing bookings during a slower season, boosting loyalty, or attracting a new demographic.

Imagine a boutique hotel launching a campaign to attract weekend travelers. Their vision of success might be defined by a spike in weekend bookings within a specific window of time. In this case, a carefully crafted social media campaign with exclusive weekend offers could serve as the primary strategy. Here, success metrics would focus on conversions—tracking the number of people who book weekend stays through the campaign link. With this clear vision, the hotel avoids chasing after likes or shares; instead, they're focused on a tangible outcome that directly affects revenue.

Now, consider a luxury resort seeking to elevate its reputation among affluent travelers. Success might look different for them: rather than immediate bookings, the campaign aims to cultivate a sense of prestige and exclusivity around the brand. In this scenario, high-quality editorial partnerships, influencer collaborations, or visually captivating content on Instagram might be prioritized to build long-term brand affinity. Here, the focus shifts to engagement metrics, such as social media impressions, reach, and perhaps the number of mentions by influential accounts. By defining success as perceived brand status rather than direct conversions, we set ourselves up for long-term gains with high-value customers who are more likely to book a stay in the future.

When beginning with defining clear, measurable objectives and selecting the right metrics to track progress, marketers ensure that every strategic decision is aligned with overarching business goals, providing a roadmap for marketing efforts.

Ask the Right Questions

To truly understand our marketing objectives, engage stakeholders in meaningful conversations beyond vague goals, like "We need more followers" or "Let's increase engagement." Start by delving deeper with questions such as:

> What specific action do we want the audience to take?

> What key message will resonate most with our target demographic?

How will we measure if the campaign is working?

Who are our primary and secondary target audiences, and what motivates them?

What is the desired timeline for achieving these goals, and how will that affect our approach?

Which marketing channels will deliver the highest impact based on our goals and audience behavior?

What potential obstacles or risks could impact the campaign's success, and how can we mitigate them?

What post-campaign actions will we take to sustain engagement and maximize ROI?

Example: A family-friendly resort initially aiming to build brand awareness may, upon deeper questioning, realize the true goal is to drive direct bookings from families seeking weekend getaways. This refined purpose directs the marketing team to focus on actionable key performance indicators (KPIs), like click-through rates to the booking page and conversion rates on family packages (actual bookings), avoiding superficial metrics like overall follower growth.

Choosing the Right KPIs for Our Goals

Once goals are clearly defined, selecting the appropriate KPIs is essential to ensure the campaign stays on track. KPIs function as navigational tools, directly linking back to objectives and providing measurable milestones of success. In the hospitality, tourism, and events sectors, the chosen KPIs will vary based on the specific experiences and outcomes you aim to deliver.

For instance, consider a charming coastal restaurant launching a campaign to boost local awareness. KPIs such as impressions, reach, and follower growth become invaluable in this scenario. These metrics demonstrate that the campaign effectively increases the restaurant's visibility among local diners. High reach and follower growth indicate that more people are discovering the restaurant and joining its audience, expanding its digital footprint. Here, the focus is on visibility rather than immediate actions, like reservations, emphasizing the importance of brand presence in the initial stages.

Conversely, imagine a winery promoting a tasting festival to foster deeper engagement. In this case, engagement metrics, such as likes, comments, and shares, take precedence. A high level of social interaction suggests that potential guests are not just passively viewing content but are actively interested, possibly even tagging friends to join them. These engagement metrics help gauge enthusiasm and word-of-mouth potential, providing insights into which posts resonate most with the audience and setting the stage for a successful event.

For campaigns centered on conversions, KPIs become more direct and action oriented. Take, for example, a boutique hotel running a campaign to drive bookings for a winter escape package, sorry, *experience*. Metrics such as click-through rates, leads generated, and actual bookings are critical in this context. If the campaign succeeds, these KPIs will confirm that people are taking the desired actions: clicking through ads, signing up for the winter getaway, and ultimately making reservations. Conversion-focused KPIs provide a direct line to revenue, making them indispensable for campaigns aimed at generating immediate financial returns.

By carefully selecting KPIs that align with specific goals, whether increasing awareness, fostering engagement, or driving conversions, we ensure our marketing efforts are strategic and measurable, leading to more effective and impactful campaigns.

Measure What Matters

Marketers today are inundated with an array of metrics, making it easy to become distracted by numbers that may not translate into meaningful business impact. To navigate this, it's crucial to prioritize metrics that directly correlate with our business objectives, ensuring that efforts are both efficient and effective.

For example, a popular tourist destination promoting a new adventure experience might find satisfaction in seeing thousands of likes on a breathtaking Instagram post. However, the real question remains: Are these likes converting into ticket sales? By focusing on click-through rates to the booking site and actual ticket purchases, the destination can assess the true impact of its social media efforts on revenue. This strategic focus ensures that resources are allocated to tactics that drive real business results rather than getting sidetracked by the allure of high social media engagement numbers.

Similarly, consider a heritage or food festival aiming to boost on-site attendance. While growing their social media following might seem like a sign of increased interest, the ultimate measure of success lies in actual ticket sales or RSVPs. By concentrating on conversion, such as ticket sales and attendee registrations, the festival can refine its campaign to emphasize messages that drive people to purchase tickets, avoiding the pitfall of investing in popular but unproductive content.

The key takeaway is that by choosing KPIs aligned with our end goals, we shift focus from accumulating vanity metrics to gathering actionable insights. This approach transforms our campaigns from creative endeavors into targeted efforts that drive meaningful business outcomes. Click-through rates, conversions, and revenue generation provide tangible evidence of the campaign's effectiveness.

Crafting a Strategy with the End in Mind

Clearly defined goals and aligned KPIs help us develop a content strategy that directly supports the objectives. This approach involves constructing each element of the campaign with the final objectives in sight, ensuring that every piece of content works toward the metrics that matter.

Take, for example, a popular beach resort aiming to increase social media engagement to build its community and encourage guest interaction. The resort can focus on interactive content, such as polls, quizzes, and user-generated photo challenges, by prioritizing engagement as the primary goal. A campaign inviting guests to share their "best beach day photos" with a branded hashtag can generate a surge of engagement, as guests feel included and excited to showcase their experiences. This strategy fosters a sense of community and drives the engagement KPIs that are essential for the resort's marketing success.

On the other hand, a new city tour company targeting direct bookings for the upcoming holiday season would adopt a different strategy. Knowing that conversions are the priority, their approach might revolve around highly targeted ads with clear calls-to-action, retargeting past visitors, and offering exclusive holiday values. Instead of focusing on content that invites casual interaction, the tour company would emphasize compelling reasons to book now, such as limited availability or time-sensitive offers (don't call it a discount!). Every element of the campaign is tailored to prompt immediate action, transforming clicks into confirmed bookings and driving the conversion KPIs that directly impact revenue. Devising a strategy with the end in mind ensures that our marketing efforts are deliberately crafted to achieve the intended KPI goals.

Budgeting Wisely from the Start

One of the first steps in any campaign is setting a clear budget that aligns with the goals. Just like we define our KPIs, knowing financial boundaries early keeps us grounded and focused. Think of the budget as the framework that guides creative decisions and strategic moves; when used smartly, it maximizes impact and avoids unnecessary spending.

For example, let's say a new farm-to-table restaurant is getting ready to launch its seasonal tasting menu, aiming to attract local food enthusiasts and influencers. By defining a modest budget from the start, the marketing team can prioritize where to invest for maximum exposure, like a well-targeted social media ad campaign or an invite-only tasting event for local bloggers. Rather than stretching thin across multiple platforms, the budget is allocated to high-impact areas that directly reach the target audience. This focused approach allows the restaurant to create buzz without going overboard on expenses like paid influencer partnerships or lavish photo shoots.

Or take the example of a small-town music festival aiming to boost ticket sales for the weekend lineup. By setting a budget early, the team can strategically invest in digital ads on local channels and create compelling social media content that reaches concertgoers in nearby areas. Defining financial limits helps avoid splurging on costly billboard ads or extensive print marketing that might sound good but don't directly impact ticket sales. Instead, the budget is dedicated to strategies that get tickets into concertgoers' hands.

Cost-Per-Acquisition Planning

When the goal is conversions, such as bookings, ticket sales, or reservations, setting a rough cost-per-conversion target can be a game-changer. This approach allows us to map a realistic budget that aligns with our end goals, ensuring we get the best return on investment (ROI) for every dollar spent.

Many companies today use cost-per-acquisition (CPA) planning for marketing budgeting, particularly in performance-driven marketing environments. This approach helps businesses allocate their marketing budgets based on desired outcomes rather than spending blindly.

How the process works:

1. **Define Clear Objectives:**

   Companies first identify what specific actions they want customers to take, such as making a purchase, subscribing to a service, signing up for a newsletter, booking a hotel room, or registering for an event. Based on these actions, they estimate the cost they are willing to pay to achieve each goal.

2. **Set Target Cost Thresholds:**

   Businesses often calculate their target cost-per-acquisition (CPA) or cost-per-lead (CPL) by considering factors such as customer lifetime value (CLV) and profit margins. For example, if a company estimates that a customer brings in $1,000 over their lifetime and wants to maintain a 10:1 return on ad spend (ROAS), they might set a cost-per-goal target of $100 per new customer.

3. **Allocate Budget Across Channels:**

   Using historical data, companies determine which channels (social media, Google Ads, email marketing, etc.) deliver the most efficient CPA and allocate their budgets accordingly.

4. **Adjust in Real Time:**

   Many companies use real-time analytics tools to monitor the CPA as a campaign runs. If a campaign is exceeding its target cost threshold without delivering enough results, it can be paused or adjusted. Or if a campaign is under the target cost, they may scale it up and invest more.

Here's how and why sectors assess CPA:

- **Hospitality and Travel:**
  Hotels and airlines frequently use CPA models to manage budgets for direct bookings. We track metrics such as cost-per-booking and cost-per-room-night to ensure campaigns deliver profitable results.

- **E-Commerce:**
  Online retailers rely heavily on cost-per-conversion or cost-per-sale to guide ad spend. Tools like Google Ads and Facebook Ads allow businesses to optimize campaigns toward a specific cost-per-goal, ensuring maximum ROI.

- **Software as a Service (SaaS):**
  SaaS companies often use cost-per-goal planning to track cost-per-trial or cost-per-sign-up with a focus on conversions (how many trial users convert to paying customers).

- **Nonprofits and Events:**
  Nonprofits running fundraising campaigns or event organizers promoting ticket sales often use this method to track cost-per-donation or cost-per-ticket-sale, ensuring their campaigns remain cost-effective.

Examples

Sharing a simplified hotel example, let's say a luxury hotel has a winter promotion to drive bookings for its wellness retreat experience. By estimating a target CPA, the hotel's marketing team can work backward to determine how much to allocate to each part of the campaign, from Google Ads to social media retargeting. If the cost-per-booking is set at $100, they know that a campaign budget of $10,000 should yield at least 100 bookings. With this target in mind, the hotel can focus its spending on high-converting channels and adjust any underperforming ads to stay within budget. It also sets a clear benchmark for evaluating the campaign's success and reallocating funds if necessary.

Equally, a tourist attraction like a popular museum might use CPA planning to maximize ticket sales for a new exhibit. Perhaps the museum aims for a cost-per-ticket-sale of $10. If they allocate $5,000 to a digital campaign, they know they should aim for 500 ticket sales to consider it a success. This method helps set financial expectations and empowers the team to be agile. If a particular ad set on social media is generating ticket sales at a lower cost, they can shift more of the budget toward it. This type of planning provides a built-in flexibility that allows marketers to adapt spending in real time.

Naturally, budgeting for any business is complicated and nuanced, and this concept is a piece of the overall puzzle.

The point is to ensure we critically think about how to make our budget work for us and remember to *keep contingency dollars aside for those always arising unexpected surprises* that surface.

Data-Driven Creativity

Data may seem like it limits creative freedom, but knowing the KPIs is helpful as we devise imaginative solutions. With clear metrics in place, teams can experiment boldly within a structured framework, using data to guide their choices. For example, a family-friendly amusement park might want to test different types of social media ads to see what drives more family group bookings. Since the goal is conversions (actual bookings), they might start by running a few A/B tests (testing two options) with various ad formats. Some might focus on video ads showcasing exciting rides and family fun, while others feature ads with ticket bundle offers. By tracking the conversion rates for each type of ad, the team can quickly spot which format resonates best with their audience, allowing them to double down on what works and phase out what doesn't.

Similarly, consider that previously-mentioned vineyard offering wine-tasting weekends, trying to increase sign-ups for its loyalty program. By setting a KPI around loyalty program conversions, they might try a series of creative campaigns that mix educational content about different wine varieties with promotions for loyalty members. Data on which post or email formats attract the most clicks or sign-ups allows the team to fine-tune their approach, balancing compelling storytelling and strategically placed calls-to-action.

This thought process extends to timing and seasonal campaigns. A ski lodge, for example, could use past data to identify peak booking periods and tailor ad strategy to these windows. This insight might inspire the team to create urgency-driven content that ramps up just before peak season, highlighting first snowfall alerts or "best weekends to ski" promotions. The creativity lies in adapting the messaging to make it as enticing as possible, all while staying grounded in the data that tells them when their audience is most likely to book.

Review and Optimize: Use Analytics to Close the Loop

When a campaign concludes, the real learning begins. The end of a campaign isn't just a stopping point; it's the start of a new cycle of insights. To ensure our marketing efforts continually improve, analyzing campaign performance against the KPIs set from the beginning is essential. By examining metrics like cost-per-acquisition and engagement rates, we see how effectively our investment paid off.

Imagine a regional food festival that runs a month-long campaign to drive ticket sales. Post-campaign analysis might show strong initial interest through social media engagement but a low conversion rate on ticket purchases. By digging into the data, the festival team may find that while engagement was high on certain platforms, direct ticket links weren't as accessible, or key calls-to-action were buried within the posts. This insight allows the team to refine their strategy for future events, ensuring ticket purchase options are front and center in high-engagement areas.

Similarly, a luxury spa resort might look at the cost-per-conversion for its holiday relaxation experience. If the cost to convert a booking was higher than expected, the team can examine where it underperformed in the marketing journey. Was it the initial ad reach, click-through rate, or on-site booking experience? By identifying exactly where the campaign was less efficient, the resort can adjust in future campaigns, reallocating budget to the highest-converting channels or simplifying the booking process for easier customer navigation.

Refine. Revise. Repeat.

Success in marketing isn't about one-hit wonders; it's about consistently iterating and improving based on what we learn. After each campaign, identify what worked well and what didn't. When something falls short—if a new restaurant's menu change fails to attract enough foot traffic, for example—take it as a signal to test alternative approaches, like reallocating ad spend to geo-targeted social ads or experimenting with a different message.

Now, think about a scenic mountain lodge that finds its "Winter Escape" promotion didn't generate the expected interest. While the ads received clicks, few visitors followed through with bookings. After reviewing the data, the lodge discovered that the offer details were vague, leaving potential guests unclear about what was included. In response, they decide to launch a follow-up campaign with more explicit descriptions and enticing imagery of cozy rooms and winter activities. By optimizing in this way, they address what held conversions back and make data-driven improvements that directly impact the next round of promotions.

Continuous improvement might also mean embracing entirely new channels or tactics based on what we learn. An urban art museum that tracks its campaign success might realize that email marketing produced more ticket sales than its usual social ads. Armed with this knowledge, the museum might shift more of its budget toward personalized email campaigns, targeting segments like local members or tourists with exhibit previews and exclusive discounts. Iteration is about knowing when to pivot based on the evidence at hand and using past performance to guide smarter, more effective future strategies.

Closing the loop with analytics and committing to iterative improvement helps us fine-tune each campaign and build a library of knowledge that strengthens every future marketing effort. This cycle of review and optimization transforms every campaign from a single effort into a lasting asset, fueling continued growth and impact for the brand.

In my classes, as we lay out the methodology of our strategic and critical thinking process with our clients, we always start with, "What is the situation? Clarify the marketing challenge." As we present the due diligence and research findings, we also assess whether the marketing challenge needs slight adjustments. When we conclude our recommendations, we end with a reminder of what the initial challenge was. This way, we can end our presentation by explaining how we started. And we started with the end goals.

Marketing Mantras

By starting with the end goals, marketers shift their mindset from reactive to proactive, ensuring that every campaign serves a clear purpose. Whether it's increasing engagement, driving revenue, or building brand loyalty, thinking like a marketer means always beginning with clarity and ending with measurable results. Remember:

1. **Define Success Clearly:**
   Start with a clear vision of the goals—whether it's conversions, brand awareness, or loyalty—and let it guide your strategy.
2. **Align Goals with Metrics:**
   Choose KPIs that directly reflect your objectives and avoid being distracted by vanity metrics.

3. **Ask Strategic Questions:**

   Go beyond surface-level goals by asking, "What do we want to achieve and why?" to uncover actionable objectives.

4. **Budget with Intent:**

   Set financial boundaries that focus on high-impact activities, ensuring every dollar aligns with your goals.

5. **Plan Backward from Goals:**

   Design your strategy and content starting with the end goal in mind to keep your efforts focused and effective.

6. **Leverage Data for Creativity:**

   Use data insights to fuel experimentation, refine campaigns, and find the sweet spot between innovation and results.

7. **Refine and Repeat:**

   Treat every campaign as a step in a continuous cycle of learning, optimization, and improvement.

Effective marketing is not just about delivering results; it's about delivering the *right* results. And our next chapter reminds us of the critical distinction between a transactional connection with customers and a relationship-driven one, emphasizing the long-term value of meaningful, trust-based relationships.

Mindset in Motion

Consider a recent project or campaign you were involved in. Reflect on how clearly defined goals influenced the outcome. What key performance indicators (KPIs) did you choose, and how did they align with your overall objectives? Think about the importance of budgeting: How did it shape your strategy from the beginning? Now, envision a new project you'd like to undertake. Start by clearly defining your end goals, then work backward to establish the necessary steps and metrics for success. Write your goals, the questions you need to ask, and the KPIs that will guide you. How will you ensure your approach remains flexible enough to refine and optimize as you learn from your data?

6

From Transactions to Trust: Building Relationships

I t is my opinion that, in the world of marketing, the most successful strategies stem from a collaborative approach where the focus shifts from "me" to "we." This element of a marketing mindset underscores the importance of partnership and collective effort when working with clients. Rather than viewing clients merely as recipients of services, they should be seen as integral collaborators to achieve shared goals. This "we" mentality fosters trust, encourages open communication, and ensures both the marketer and the client are aligned in their vision and objectives.

By embracing a collaborative approach, marketers can create more effective, relevant campaigns, reflecting the needs and aspirations of their clients. Adopting a relationship-driven approach transforms marketing from a series of one-off transactions into a continuous dialogue.

I also know that the most successful opportunities and partnerships thrive because they are rooted in meaningful and sincere relationships. When interactions are handled transactionally (focused solely on immediate gains or outcomes), they often lack authenticity and fail to foster trust. True connection requires effort, empathy, and a genuine investment in understanding and supporting one another. Simple shifts in language, like saying "We are in this together" instead of "You need to do the following," emphasize collaboration and reinforce that we are all working on the same team. Relationships, like anything worthwhile, take time and care to build; through this deliberate cultivation, they become highly valued and enduring.

Classroom Cases

Here are a few memories of situations where the use of "we" rather than "you" or "I" formed a lasting impression on our classroom clients:

Marketing a Modern Tavern with a Historic Twist

Student: Theresa Hughes

School: BU School of Hospitality Administration

Graduation: Class of 2023

The Marketing Challenge: Punch Bowl opened in April 2021 in the lobby of the (then) new Hilton Garden Inn in Brookline Village, Massachusetts. It was the latest offering from locally renowned restaurateurs, Jen and Josh Ziskin. Inspired by the historic eighteenth-century tavern Brookline was once famous for, the Ziskins "rekindled the spirit of the Punch Bowl and have recreated a communal gathering place in the heart of the village."

In the 1700s, the original Punch Bowl Tavern was located at Brookline's Hearthstone Plaza, where travelers passed by and gathered on their journey through Boston. Punch Bowl Brookline has taken a modern twist on a city tavern. Chef Josh prepares cuisine featuring his contemporary take on traditional New England fare and focuses on various local farms and seafood. The initial challenges we were presented with were to increase awareness, engage with the community, and increase private events.

Outcome: Upon analyzing the competitors, speaking to numerous primary sources, and scouring relevant secondary research, the team centered their mission around history, gathering, and togetherness. One of the message highlights was an emphasis on Jen's all-female-vintner wine list inspired by the female innkeepers of the late 1700s. Jen reached out to the student team in hopes of hiring one of them to execute the plan.

By emphasizing shared values and engaging with the local community, the team successfully positioned Punch Bowl as more than a restaurant; they positioned it as a communal gathering place rooted in history and trust.

Theresa's Insight: "From day one of our class, we learned the value of relationship building. To build impactful relationships with clients, we were guided about the importance of using intentional communication.

"Now, after graduating from BU, I have quickly come to understand the significance of communication in fostering trusting relationships. In an industry where I am constantly communicating with clients, the lesson of utilizing 'we' instead of 'you' has become a golden rule in my day-to-day interactions.

"At the beginning of my role as a digital marketing analyst, the senior team made it a point for everyone to utilize 'we' instead of 'you' in client calls with general managers. One of the first training initiatives I experienced in this role involved the higher-ups recording all our client calls and conversations to hear where we have opportunities to strengthen the relationships in our conversations. The bosses came back to us and said, 'Please refer to your clients and say 'we' not 'you.' For example, indicate 'We're in this together' or 'This is what *we* need to do,' rather than saying, 'I've identified an opportunity, and here's how you can handle it.' This ensures our hotel clients know we're on their side. We're on the same team.

"Our weekly calls include various departments such as revenue, digital, operations, sales, and managers. Given the diversity of our team, it is crucial for us to speak cohesively as one unit. Whenever I discuss our digital strategy, I make a conscious effort to communicate as a team by using '*we*.' Particularly when discussing ways to improve, I ensure to begin with a compliment (another lesson from our classes) before proposing how to collaborate to enhance our digital presence.

"Over time, this approach has become second nature and allowed me to feel confident in building strong relationships in the workplace."

Reimagining Lunchtime: Elevating Outlook Kitchen's Daytime Appeal

Student: Mingjing He

School: BU School of Hospitality Administration

Graduation: Class of 2019 and MSc in Data Science from ESSEC 2025

The Marketing Challenge: The Envoy Hotel's Outlook Kitchen was a casual, upscale restaurant featuring the flavors of Executive Chef (and Food Network frequent guest) Tatiana Rosana. The restaurant's locally sourced food combined with global ingredients to form an enriching taste. Established in 2015, the restaurant had been successful during dinner hours and weekends but had not found the same success for weekday lunches. Due to rapid community development and increased options for diners, Outlook Kitchen was pushed to elevate its lunch strategy to remain competitive and relevant. Outlook's primary challenge was to attract foot traffic during weekday lunches and to achieve increased revenue.

Outcome: The student team provided detailed, research-based recommendations for increasing Outlook's physical and digital awareness in and around the Seaport neighborhood of Boston. The effort targeted working professionals who dined out for lunch frequently during the week. The recommendations coincided with strategies to gain business in three segments: in-house business lunch, delivery, and corporate catering, all to increase weekday lunch revenues.

The students' approach highlighted the importance of understanding customer behavior and preferences, fostering stronger connections between the restaurant and its patrons.

Mingjing's Insight: "When rehearsing for the final presentation in the strategic marketing course, one comment continued to surface in nearly every team feedback session: the use of 'we' instead of 'you,' particularly when delivering recommendations to our clients. This approach emphasizes that we are working together to improve a marketing issue. After college, I have used the word 'we' even more often during my job as a hotel consultant. My clients seem to have more trust in me when they know I am on their team."

I recall that when this team presented to my friend, General Manager Joe Mellia, his first comment in congratulating the team was, "Thank you for using 'we' and assuring me that we were in this together. I appreciate that you put yourself into my team as you developed these ideas. Thank you."

If You Can't Bring Them to Boston, How Do We Bring Boston to Them?

Student: Lawrence Mannix

School: BU School of Hospitality Administration

Graduation: Class of 2021

The Marketing Challenge: In the fall of 2020, the world was haunted by a global pandemic. Classes were held on-site with masks. I was eager to help the city of Boston in any way I possibly could, so I asked the Convention and Visitors Bureau (now Meet Boston) CEO, Martha Sheridan, if we could work with the city to assist with tourism marketing during this very precarious time. I'm grateful for her trust in our class and her willingness to hear from students. If we can't bring visitors to Boston because of the travel restrictions, how can we bring Boston to the visitors to foster and retain connection?

Outcome: The student team addressed the relevance of driving Boston staycation bookings into 2021 and designed a campaign for the suddenly slow period, of course respecting the guidelines of the pandemic and the varying levels of comfort from visitors and their possible fear of travel. Martha's comments to the students at the conclusion of their presentation were memorable: "I've worked with student groups from other schools throughout my career, but this team, you really know who we are, how we speak, how we connect, and what we want to accomplish. These recommendations are actionable and 'on brand.'"

Suggestions included the use of specific virtual tours, highlighting the diversity of the city's neighborhoods, and led by micro-influencers. The students went a step further, recommending specific influencers and explaining their rationale. Online experiences and events, including New England-style cooking classes, were also suggested, all under the campaign hashtag of #BringBostonHome.

The students also suggested a banner across the homepage of BostonUSA.com, sharing the travel advisory updates, with messages of "See you soon in Boston" to keep the communication engaged. And of course, that came with approaches to get visitors to the website in the first place.

By focusing on meaningful engagement and community connection, the students' campaign strengthened

Boston's relationship with potential visitors even during a time of enormous travel restrictions.

Lawrence's Insight: "I remember the concept of a team environment fondly as an important learning technique. Structuring our classroom as a marketing agency and working as supportive rather than competitive teams was healthy and made the marketing brainstorming sessions more fun. My team's client was the CEO of Boston's destination marketing agency, and I specifically recall her incredible reaction because we performed as a unified team and demonstrated that we were also part of her team. She said, 'You got us. You really understood what we're about.'"

Turning Valleys into Opportunities: A Strategic Push for Off-Season Bookings

Student: Elise Borkan Mackin

School: BU School of Hospitality Administration

Graduation: Class of 2019

The Marketing Challenge: A typical hotel marketing challenge is to focus on increasing leisure bookings during the shoulder season or off-peak ("valley") periods. In 2019, in Boston, these slower occupancy times were January, February, and the United States holiday seasons, including Easter, Fourth of July, Thanksgiving, and Christmas. At the time, the Fairmont Copley Plaza hotel in Back Bay possessed a market mix of approximately 60 percent leisure and 40 percent business travelers. The hotel relied heavily on the leisure travel market and believed it was imperative to market to leisure travelers during slow months.

Outcome: The strategy to increase leisure bookings during the valley periods resulted in a two-pronged approach, named by the student team as "Fairmont Experiences" and "Fairmont Holidays" (designed specifically for those times of the year). Designed to create distinctive and memorable times for guests, the marketing efforts for Fairmont Experiences involved Google advertising, social media advertising, and video content creation. Fairmont Holidays' marketing approaches sought to enhance the booking process, implement video content marketing, and schedule social media advertising.

The three target personas developed for this effort were millennial couples without children, baby boomer couples not traveling with kids, and families with young children. Thus, the experiences were created for each of the target personas, supplemented by imagery to project these personas. The targeted experiences included "Boston for Two," "Historic Hub," and "Fairmont Families," and all could be tailored to the customers' liking. Pop-ups on the website, retargeting of digital ads, recommendations for keywords to use on the website (organic), and paid search initiatives geotargeted within a fifty-mile radius of Boston.

A digital assessment of the hotel's web pages revealed very long load speeds for numerous webpages (which fortunately were easy fixes for the web developer) and the need to increase video content and rich media on the website. (Rich media refers to digital content with advanced features such as video, audio or interactive elements, to engage users more deeply.) The team also suggested a social media partnership with the famed Boston Pops leading up to the July Fourth celebration.

Elise's Insight: "The concept of 'I' and 'we' is a strong one. We behaved as consultants in class; now, I work with country club members. I need to say 'we' because they are dues-paying members, and we are in this together. This is a great practice, and I continue it today. Additionally, community connections are important, and we learned this from our projects."

It's not "you." It's "we."

These student mini-marketing cases illustrate the power of collaboration, creativity, and strategic thinking in addressing real-world challenges. From positioning a modern tavern as a communal gathering space rooted in history to reimagining lunch strategies for a casual upscale restaurant, each example highlights the importance of understanding customer needs and fostering connections.

Whether driving local tourism during a global pandemic or creating targeted experiences to boost leisure bookings, these cases also show how thoughtful, research-driven approaches can generate actionable solutions. And, they reinforce the value of using "we" instead of "you," emphasizing the role of teamwork and relationship-building in successful marketing strategies.

> I'm even trying to project a tone of "we" throughout this book. I want to convey that, as marketers, we are in this together.

Relationship Building

Authenticity Matters

I genuinely believe it is critical for Gen Z and the rising Alpha generation to learn, understand, and appreciate the concept of relationship-building from more seasoned professionals. Excellence in work quality is fundamental (this should be the baseline), but it's only the beginning. Earning trust through consistent, high-quality efforts paves the way for respect and great working relationships with colleagues. These relationships can blossom into strong friendships enduring beyond the confines of a single job, spanning entire careers, even lasting a lifetime.

Authentic relationships, rather than transactional ones, provide substantial benefits. Transactional interactions are often short-lived, focused on immediate needs, and lack the depth needed to build trust and form genuine connections. True relationships, however, are built on mutual respect, trust, and a commitment to excellence and each other's success, leading to enduring and meaningful connections. Hospitality as an industry, perhaps more than any other, is built on the strength of relationships. Each job move and connection for business success is strengthened thanks to previously developed trustworthy relationships.

This principle applies equally to brands and marketing. Our goal is to ensure our brands—whether they are companies, products, services, or causes—forge trusted relationships with our customers. Every touchpoint should enhance this trust, fostering a deeper connection. Customers' loyalty and trust grow as they interact with the brand, transforming a simple transaction into an evolving, meaningful relationship.

Building Trust Over Time

I held two simultaneous internships while in graduate school, when I started my career. One was with the Four Seasons at the Boston Common, which had just opened. My work quality and proactive efforts to connect with colleagues and managers developed into trusting relationships, leading to my next job with Sheraton Hotels in New York. My relationships were completely organic and were the outcome of who I am as a human, a hospitality-minded individual. When relationships are built on authenticity and trust, they are treasured. When people no longer work together at the same company, relationships take work. We must make the effort to stay in touch and see each other whenever possible. Social media connections are tremendously helpful. Work and social friends from years ago still feel close, as if no time has passed—thanks to the way online connection keeps us in each other's lives. Genuine friendships and professional support yield continuous success in each other's next roles. So, deliver quality work, build trust and genuine friendships, and make the effort to keep the relationship fresh. It's important for personal and professional enrichment and achievement.

Building trust and fostering authentic relationships are at the heart of successful marketing. In the Row 34 case below, Marut and his team demonstrate how inclusive communication and collaboration created a sense of shared purpose, empowering stakeholders and delivering impactful digital strategies. Similarly, Chloe and her team's work with Rochambeau exemplifies the importance of a collective mindset, positioning her team as true partners to their client and adapting seamlessly to the challenges of the moment.

Staying Afloat:
Assessing Digital Visibility in a Sea of New Competitors

Student: Marut K. Raval

School: BU School of Hospitality Administration

Graduation: Class of 2020, MMH (Master of Management in Hospitality) Class of 2021

The Marketing Challenge: When Marut was the teaching assistant for my digital marketing course in the Spring of 2020, we had the wonderful opportunity to conduct a digital assessment for one of Boston's premier seafood restaurants, Row 34. Located in Boston's Seaport neighborhood, the Boston Wharf Company textile warehouse was first built in 1908 and became the original Row 34 in 2013. Since then, the vibe is energetic, whether at the bar, on the patio, or at a private event in the Cooler Room. Claiming the city's best lobster roll, Row 34 is led by famed chef, partner, and cookbook author Jeremy Sewall, who began his training at the Culinary Institute of America. With new seafood establishments rapidly coming into the market, it was time to review the restaurant's digital footprint and understand what elements needed enhancement for a stronger online presence.

The Outcome: Students reviewed the digital presence of three competitive sets to make elevated recommendations. Comp Set 1 consisted of other seafood restaurants. Comp Set 2 included competitors for the bar scene and selection of beers available, and Comp Set 3 was composed of comparable businesses with event spaces that accommodated similar-sized groups. This was a smart approach to determine the keywords to optimize and help the restaurant strengthen its messaging compared with other restaurants, bars, or event spaces.

The students researched various elements of the iconic restaurant's digital footprint:

Are the online menus in HTML or PDF, which are not ideal for SEO purposes?

Were prices indicated online?

Did the site list the beer offerings?

Did competitors have private spaces and stronger photography?

How's the overall website user experience? The use of links? The Google My Business page? (Also for SEO purposes.)

Did the restaurant respond to online comments via travel sites, online reputation sites, or social media?

The class also worked beautifully together to design a deck template reflecting the restaurant's visual branding. We conducted rehearsals so each team (competitive set, website user experience, paid search and email marketing, SEO, ORM [online reputation management], and social media) could present and use transitions to seamlessly connect to the next team. The student groups collaborated to ensure the entire presentation resulted in what I call a "well-choreographed ballet." In the semester when the pandemic erupted, the class quickly had to pivot to rehearse online, learn how to present through Zoom, and even wear a unified look for tops and blouses, so we all were in presentation mode to deliver our findings and suggestions through a screen.

Marut's Insight: "A life lesson I'm glad to have learned in class is that everything is relationship-driven. I've found this to be especially relevant as I've progressed in my career in the commercial real estate industry. Using inclusive language ('we') helps when speaking with external parties. It shares the sense that we are all on the same team, and I have noticed that negotiations tend to go smoother when utilizing this type of language. This is also helpful when dealing with internal stakeholders. I almost always use 'we' when speaking with my team at work. I never want anyone to become defensive, especially if I'm delivering critical feedback. We're all on the same team, and I want people to feel it. It makes collaboration smoother."

Cuisine to Camera: Video Series to Share a French Restaurant's Story and Invite New Guests

Student: Chloe Brendlinger

School: BU School of Hospitality Administration

Graduation: Class of 2020

The Marketing Challenge: One assignment in our digital course was to create a three-part video content marketing series conveying a solid theme and overarching campaign for an individual restaurant. The ability to storyboard messaging, determine b-roll and interview shots, clip them together, and create content useful for social media or website SEO purposes is a terrific hands-on skill for our marketers. Stories and messages were set, filming (with iPhones, mind you) had begun, and then the world suddenly stopped in March 2020. However, the assignment continued. And this was a lesson in pivoting, crisis and change management, and using one's sense of resourcefulness to shift gears.

Outcome: Chloe's team focused on the Lyons Group French restaurant, Rochambeau. What started as a three-part video series about the energetic and party-like atmosphere of the relatively new dining establishment had to suddenly shift gears with a simple, more low-key awareness campaign, highlighting to-go offerings to meet the sudden needs of the time.

Chloe's Insight: "We learned that when working as a team and with clients, it's always about 'we.' Also in marketing, it's crucial to speak collectively rather than individually. In our presentations, we learned to use 'ours' instead of 'yours,' demonstrating we see their challenges as our own. We position ourselves as an extension of their team. This approach is something I apply daily with clients at the hospitality marketing agency where I work."

These two examples show that building trust and fostering authentic relationships are essential for successful marketing initiatives. In the Row 34 project, Marut and his team's inclusive communication and collaborative approach ensured that all stakeholders felt valued and engaged. Similarly, Chloe's team for Rochambeau emphasized a collective "we" mindset, positioning themselves as true extensions of their client's team and facilitating seamless adaptation and meaningful content creation even during challenging times.

Professional to Personal

Julie Freeman is executive vice president for the Americas of MMGY Global, a premier international travel marketing organization. Julie and I are both active members of HSMAI (the Hospitality Sales and Marketing Association International), and I spoke with her for the spring edition of our school's *Boston Hospitality Review.* Julie reminds us that the trust placed in us as marketers is based on strong and healthy relationships:

"The media landscape is constantly shifting and evolving. Publicists and marketers should continue to be at the forefront, trying new technologies, platforms, apps, etc., and figuring out how these can be incorporated into strategies. Travel marketers must remain nimble in our media relations strategies to cost-effectively target a narrowing pool of influential writers and platforms by prioritizing relationship-building. This includes increased collaboration with freelance contributors, embracing niche outlets, championing new content platforms, and implementing proven syndication techniques for creative storytelling."

Denise Dupre, founder and managing partner of Champagne Hospitality, was my thesis advisor in graduate school; she was director of BU's School of Hospitality at the time. Many moons later, Denise is a Dean's Advisory Board member at the BU School of Hospitality. She built a hotel in Epernay, France, and owns a nearby champagne cellar. I had the good fortune of teaching in Paris for BU one summer, and I had asked Denise if we could bring a group of students to visit her locations there. My goal was to create a memorable experience for those students, and I can comfortably say we succeeded. Authentic relationships in our industry are professional connections and can genuinely evolve into sincere friendships, grounded in mutual trust rather than mere transactions. I treasure these relationships, which enrich both my personal and professional life.

Meaningful Community Connections

In today's times, fostering strong relationships with local communities is more essential than ever. These connections enhance the guest experience and create a sense of belonging that resonates deeply with travelers. By actively engaging with local businesses, artists, and organizations, hospitality establishments can enrich offerings and showcase the inimitable culture of their surroundings. This collaboration not only supports local economies but also builds brand loyalty, as guests increasingly seek authentic experiences that reflect the spirit of the destination. Ultimately, nurturing these relationships transforms hospitality businesses into integral parts of the communities they serve, creating a symbiotic partnership that benefits all. This is genuine public relations.

From Local Ties to Lasting Loyalty

Student: Teagan Lucchese

School: BU School of Hospitality Administration

Graduation: Class of 2023

The Marketing Challenge: To identify recommendations for enhancing the online presence of Punch Bowl, a restaurant concept within the Hilton Garden Inn in Brookline, Massachusetts. The objective was to expand Punch Bowl's digital footprint and elevate its social media engagement by fostering connections with the Brookline community and increasing private event bookings.

Outcome: As part of their research and due diligence, the team spoke directly with Candace MacDonald, managing director of Carbonate, a brand communications and services agency specializing in food, beverage, and hospitality. Candace speaks to my classes periodically to share food and beverage (F&B) trends across the United States. At this time, Carbonate observed four specific F&B trends: seafood cocktails, tiered plating, cocktails for group dining, and "plenty of spirit. No alcohol."

Teagan's Insight: "I frequently encounter the 'relationship versus transactional' dynamic in my current role. As restaurants are driven by human interactions with colleagues and guests, the quality of these interactions defines whether they evolve into relationships or remain mere transactions. I have learned how nurturing the community is crucial to a restaurant's success. A supportive community is an essential asset, and cultivating meaningful relationships with it can significantly enhance a restaurant's impact and reputation. Whether I knew it at the time or not, the concept of community was central to Punch Bowl's success—and at the heart of our digital marketing challenge and project.

"Additionally, the impression you have after visiting a restaurant or service establishment largely depends on your interactions with the team members. It's crucial that guests feel good and emotionally fulfilled after their experience; this is a key indicator of exceptional hospitality. My company emphasizes the distinction between service and hospitality: Service is transactional and emotionless, while hospitality fosters relationships and evokes feelings. How we make others feel distinguishes us and reassures clients we are on their side, embodying a 'we' rather than 'you' relationship. This was a major challenge at the start of our project, given the restaurant's location inside a hotel lobby. We had to consider, 'How can we (Punch Bowl) leave a lasting impression on guests who may not be local?' This sparked one of our key strategies in the digital marketing project—surprisingly, email marketing. To this day, I still receive Punch Bowl's email blasts, which keep me emotionally connected and remind me of my dining experience.

"The lessons learned from the Punch Bowl initiative parallel my current role in restaurants. Ultimately, it's the impressions we leave and the relationships we build that define a great partnership with our clients."

Beyond Burritos and Beers: A Deep Dive into Elevating a Campus Mexican Restaurant's Online Image

Student: Lucas Topper

School: BU School of Hospitality Administration

Graduation: MMH Class of 2023

The Marketing Project: Sunset Cantina, a much-loved go-to spot on the Boston University campus referred to as "Sunset," features affordable Mexican food and a respectable array of beers and cocktail offerings. Owner Catarina Chang, a School of Hospitality Administration alum, asked for a specific assessment of her digital marketing initiatives; she wanted an outside set of eyes to review her restaurant's digital footprint.

Outcome: Using Similarweb.com, teams could determine the number of monthly web visitors, unique visitors, and the bounce rate (measuring the percentage of unengaged visitors to a site). Using the same site, the students could also compare the SERP placement (search engine results page—where your business lands when someone conducts a Google search), the length of time visitors spent on the site, and the average number of web pages visited.

The mobile site navigation was also thoroughly reviewed. The mobile site fared well thanks to large enough text and links for fluid usability. The pinch-to-zoom functionality of photos was also enabled and was effective for users. The speed of each page was also strong.

The students suggested a stronger color contrast on the site for a more effective adherence to ADA guidelines. The students also recommended the use of more significant keywords for searchers to find the site and to include copy and imagery to depict the event space. SEO would be enhanced by improving meta descriptions[5] on webpages. Email marketing with pop-up forms, a Facebook page with the ability to sign up for the newsletter, and tighter and stronger subject lines for newsletters were also among the paid search suggestions. A social media calendar for TikTok, Instagram, and Facebook posts was recommended, along with suggestions for additional strong photography. Guidance was also provided to explain how influencers could be converted into frequent guests.

Lucas's Insight: "This project revealed a deeper perspective on marketing; rather than viewing it as merely transactional (i.e., 'What can you do for me?'), I learned to see it as relational and impactful, for example, 'How can you shape my lens?' This approach emphasizes nurturing a relationship rather than just completing a transaction.

"Through this project, I gained a deeper understanding of what drives customer decisions and how a brand's communication and marketing efforts can be both personal and personalized. This experience has been invaluable in my role in B2B marketing for a hospitality tech company.

"In an industry often characterized by transactional marketing, I draw on this classroom experience to adopt a customer-centric approach. Rather than merely listing numbers or facts, I build and nurture relationships with our clients. This approach differentiates our brand and fosters long-term loyalty and engagement while positioning the organization as a thought leader."

Best Practices for Strong Relations

Can professional relationships evolve into personal friendships? Relationships and trust mean you can call someone at a moment's notice to review another person's resume or receive a piece of advice. The deeper the relationship, the more honest and authentic the connection can become. Someone can take many simple and easy steps to help build their professional connections and convey trust and friendship. I continually guide my students to consider the following principles:

- **Express Gratitude:**

  It's important to thank a guest lecturer for visiting the class. This helps expand your global network and begins to project your personal brand as someone who cares. If connecting on LinkedIn, remember that when connecting through a mobile device, you need to take the extra step of sending a thank-you message. LinkedIn connecting is not thanking. It's simply adding a connection. Consider a hand-written thank-you card to separate yourself from others.

- **Avoid Immediate Requests:**

  I find it irresponsible to ask for a job or for internship opportunities when you've just met the contact. Even when individuals are alums of the same program, please don't expect that because you have the school in common, you'll be the first to get the internship or job. It's important to demonstrate your work quality, humanity, and integrity to build a relationship of trust. Approach relationships with a focus on genuine connection rather than immediate gain.

- **Maintain Communication:**

  Stay in touch with people. It's not easy, but it's important. To know someone with whom you've worked in the past is on your radar, and you are on theirs, is critical. This helps when reaching out for work opportunities or to recommend others. Stay in touch. Make the effort. It takes work, but the work becomes fun because the relationships become trusted friends beyond work colleagues. If you read an article that makes you think about someone, text them and tell them. Say hi. If you saw a movie and you know someone who would enjoy it, let them know. There are easy ways to stay in touch. LinkedIn and Facebook help us by telling us daily who is having a work anniversary or birthday. Reach out and congratulate. Share something personal. Keep the friendship alive.

- **Embrace the Spirit of Hospitality:**
  Hospitality is an industry about people, travel, experiences, and global connections. Deliver excellence in your work. Earn trust, and you will have work friends who will assist when you need guidance, opportunity, or references. Strive to build a solid reputation and earn trust, and you'll cultivate a network of friends worldwide who are ready to offer guidance, opportunities, or references when needed.

By following these practices, professionals can cultivate lasting relationships that enhance their personal networks and drive sustained business success.

Marketing Mantras

1. **Adopt a Collaborative Mindset:**
   The most effective marketing strategies emerge from a collaborative mindset, where clients are viewed as partners rather than mere recipients of services. This partnership approach fosters stronger engagement and better outcomes.

2. **Build Relationships on Respect and Trust:**
   Lasting professional and personal bonds are built on a foundation of authenticity, mutual respect, and trust. Strong relationships lead to greater loyalty and long-term success.

3. **Express Gratitude and Stay Connected:**

   Simple gestures like expressing gratitude and maintaining regular communication can significantly expand your network and strengthen trust over time.

4. **Focus on Value, Not Transactions:**

   Avoid transactional requests that prioritize short-term gain. Instead, focus on demonstrating genuine value and building meaningful connections that grow over time.

5. **Prioritize Relationships, for any Business, Particularly in Hospitality:**

   In the hospitality industry, relationships are paramount. Strong reputations and trusted connections form the foundation for long-term success, making relationship-building an essential skill for marketers and leaders alike.

Building authentic relationships forms the heart of successful marketing and business development. We create a foundation that supports long-term growth and collaboration by fostering trust, respect, and genuine connections. However, strong relationships alone aren't enough; effective marketers must also cultivate and communicate their distinct value. In the next chapter, we shift our focus to "The Brand of You"—how to define, position, and market yourself with the same strategic thinking used for businesses and products.

Mindset in Motion

Think about a brand or business you deeply trust. What actions have they taken over time to earn your loyalty? Now, focus on your professional relationships with clients, colleagues, or customers. How have you built trust in these relationships? Identify one specific way you can move a transactional inter-action toward a more meaningful, trust-based connection. Consider authenticity, consistency, and personal engagement. What small but intentional step can you take today to strengthen a relationship and build lasting loyalty?

Marketing Mindset Scorecard
Track Your Progress and Develop a Thoughtful Marketing Mindset

This scorecard is designed to help you assess your growth as you read *Marketing Mindset: Lessons from Hospitality*. By reflecting on the key concepts of the previous six chapters, we gain a deeper understanding that marketing is a strategic discipline. With a hospitality-driven approach, it is also an essential business mindset.

How to Use This Scorecard:

- **Self-assess:**
  At the end of each section, rate yourself on a scale from 1 to 5 in the designated categories.

- **Reflect:**

  Consider the questions under each milestone to gauge how well you're applying the concepts.

- **Evolve:**

  Adjust your marketing mindset as you progress, revisiting earlier chapters when necessary.

Cultivating the Marketing Mindset: Critical and Strategic Thinking

Chapters 1–6

Milestone: From Awareness to Strategic Thinking

Concept	1 (Needs Work)	3 (Getting There)	5 (Fully Integrated)
Thinking Like a Marketer, Acting Like an Owner	I focus on tactics, not strategy	I consider ROI, but struggle to connect tactics to strategy	I align marketing with business objectives and ROI
Understanding Your Why	I market without a clear purpose	I see the importance of why, but struggle to define it	I start every strategy with a clear purpose

Brand and Experience Connection	I view branding as a logo or slogan	I recognize the role of customer experience in branding	I build brands with experiences that reinforce authenticity
Strategic Goal Setting	I set vague goals without measurement	I track goals but struggle with meaningful KPIs	I define clear, measurable goals and refine them based on data

Reflection Questions:

- Have you shifted from executing tactics to thinking about long-term strategy?
- Can you articulate the why behind a brand's marketing strategy?
- Are you considering customer experience as a core part of your brand positioning?

PART II

Marketing Yourself

7

The Brand of You

ersonal branding has emerged as a critical tool for distinguishing yourself both personally and professionally. Whether you are aspiring to advance in your industry, transition to a new career, or simply enhance your professional presence, understanding and cultivating your personal brand is essential. It builds trust, fosters meaningful relationships, and creates lasting impressions that open doors to new opportunities and sustained career success. In this chapter, we delve into the principles of personal branding, exploring how to define your unique identity and strategically present yourself across various platforms.

A Story of Professional Personal Branding

During my time at HVS, my colleagues Jim Houran (a hospitality-centric leadership advisor), Eydie Shapiro (who intelligently brought her hotel operations and marketing background to the field of home healthcare), and I visited the La Samanna Resort. Then part of the Orient Express brand and today a jeweled Belmond Hotel, the resort is "perched on one of the most spectacular private beaches in the French West Indies. This gorgeous hotel features fifty-one suites, twenty-five rooms, and eight villas, each with captivating views of the Caribbean Sea (I can attest to that) alongside two very inviting swimming pools. We were there to train the sales managers on the use of social media for prospecting and projecting the hotel brand while sharing the cautions that come with commenting so publicly on social platforms. (This was in 2012-ish, when social media was just becoming useful for lead generation.) The message Eydie and I kept repeating to the luxury hotel sales professionals was, "You are the convergence of your personal and professional brand." What did we mean by this?

In the early days of Facebook and long before Instagram or even before LinkedIn emerged as a dominant professional networking platform, some executives, including me, tried to establish a Facebook page for my personal photos and posts and a separate one for my professional insights. Two Facebook profiles were very difficult to manage and caused too much stress. Ultimately, my posts blended into one feed, which meant that if I wanted to share opinions on politics or education, or even on hospitality and criticisms of hotel brands, I had to think twice before I posted. This reflects my brand, and frankly, also reflects the company I work for. Now, not everyone agrees with this philosophy today, and not everyone seems to care, but I come from the mindset that what I project about my personal beliefs publicly impacts how I'm viewed professionally. I am the convergence of my personal and professional brands.

Eydie and I guided the sales team on how to prospect using social media and retain private mode (or not) when prospecting. We also explained how their posts could impact what a potential customer would think about them because you are the combination of your personal and professional brands.

This is about "The Brand of You."

Reflections and Recollections: The Brand of You

Here are several insights from former students reflecting on the significance of cultivating their personal brand and how it has shaped their personal and professional journeys.

"Our class lesson titled 'What's Your Why?' encouraged marketers and owners to dig deep and think about the true reason for the creation of their company and offerings, taking into consideration personal and organizational goals to explain the purpose of a brand's existence. An invaluable takeaway was understanding that a brand encompasses tangible and intangible elements defining its image.

"I recall this lesson often, even today, because it influences how I present myself both personally and professionally. I use this lesson to think twice about what my values are and how I want to convey them."

—Micaela Yee,
BU School of Hospitality, Class of 2023

"Our strategic marketing course discussed how our true brand lies at the intersection between our personal and professional selves. While I eventually decided to pursue a medical career, the lessons still apply. During medical school and when applying for neurosurgery residency programs, I created Instagram and Twitter accounts that I wanted my current friends, future colleagues, and patients to know. This brand of 'Jovanna' represents: (1) a doctor who is professional and will advocate for her patients; (2) a colleague who is a good friend, well-rounded with a life outside of work, and will be easy to work with; and (3) a physician-scientist who is curious and motivated to further patient care.

"I am now much more comfortable with projecting myself as a single 'brand' when connecting with friends, future employers, and patients."

—Jovanna Fazzini Tracz,
BU School of Hospitality, Class of 2016

"You are the connection of your personal and professional brand. This philosophy has profoundly impacted my career, especially in acting and entrepreneurship. In acting, honing my personal brand has been essential. I've had to understand what makes me unique while also paying attention to how the industry perceives me and the roles I'm suited for. Balancing self-awareness and external feedback allows for a dynamic and authentic personal brand. The insights from our classes together have been invaluable in navigating this mix of personal and professional identity."

—Corinne Ognibene,
BU School of Hospitality, Class of 2017

"During the strategic marketing classes, we were working on our final project for the restaurant, Golden Spoon. While developing the marketing plan and during our visit to the restaurant, we realized how strong the owner's brand truly was (Fafa is her name); it was evident through reviews and comments that customers loved and admired Fafa herself. We reviewed some of our lessons on branding, and key points included 'building an aspirational brand,' 'having a core belief that is authentic to the brand,' and 'relationships are the lifeblood of brands.' These lessons led us to recommend to Fafa that she build her storytelling and restaurant brand around her core values and dreams. It was a natural."

—Harsh Gohite,
ESSEC IMHI, Class of 2024

"We learned how to develop and communicate our individual brands, and that was precious and helpful. Small initiatives leave large impressions. For example, we were encouraged to research our guest speakers before their visits and then reach out to them with a simple thank-you message after their presentation. I never used to do that before, and it felt so uncomfortable for me. But it got easier as I practiced and kept that habit; now, I always do it. The email signature is another personal brand element that we focused on. All these tiny steps helped me gain confidence professionally. This helps me market myself."

—Johanna Reboullet,
ESSEC IMHI, Class of 2024

"I will always appreciate the connections we made with our guest speakers in our marketing classes. I advise students and anyone, for that matter, not to be intimidated by senior-level executives in hospitality or marketing. They come to class because they want to help you. Do not be afraid to speak with any of the guests; they could be your next boss or partner. Learn how to project your brand and market yourself."

—Lawrence Mannix,
BU School of Hospitality, Class of 2021

Crafting Your Unique Identity: Conscious Marketing of Yourself

Personal branding has become more than just a buzzword; it's a strategic differentiator for success in both personal and professional realms. Your personal brand encompasses how you present yourself to the world, the perceptions others have of you, and the reputation you cultivate over time. Every action, interaction, and decision you make shapes your brand, making it essential to proactively manage and cultivate your identity. From the reflections shared above, here's what we learned to consider:

1. **Self-Awareness and Appreciation of Your Strengths:**

   Understanding who you are is the foundation of personal branding. Begin with deep self-reflection to assess your values, strengths, skills, passions, and unique qualities that set you apart. This self-awareness establishes credibility and helps you recognize opportunities that align with your authentic self and long-term goals. For example, Jovanna Fazzini Tracz defined her brand as a professional and approachable physician-scientist, balancing expertise with a personable demeanor, which guided her career choices and professional interactions.

2. **An Authentic and Professional Presence:**
   Maintain consistency and authenticity in your actions, behaviors, and communications across all platforms and encounters. Acting with integrity builds trust and reinforces your brand's reliability. Demonstrate professionalism through punctuality, reliability, and respectful interactions while upholding high ethical standards. This combination ensures that others perceive you as trustworthy, dependable, and ethically sound, fostering positive relationships in both academic and professional settings. For instance, Harsh Gohite's team recommended that a restaurant owner build storytelling around her core values and dreams, reinforcing authenticity and trust with her customers.

3. **Your Digital Footprint and Expression of Thought Leadership:**
   In today's digital times, your online presence is a critical aspect of your personal brand. Curate your profiles on social media, professional networking sites, and personal websites to reflect your brand values and identity. Maintain a consistent and professional image to reach a broader audience and reinforce your personal brand. Additionally, showcase your expertise and personality by creating and sharing valuable content through blog posts, articles, videos, or social media updates. Content creation positions you as a thought leader in your field, while curated content from

reputable sources further establishes your authority and engages your audience. For example, if you market a luxury urban hotel ideal for upscale weddings, you might consider revitalizing the hotel's website and social media to position the property as a forward-thinking venue for modern weddings, demonstrating thought leadership through strategic content.

4. **Effective Networking and Relationship-Building:**

    Cultivate meaningful connections with peers, mentors, and industry professionals by engaging in networking events, conferences, and online communities. Building strong relationships supports your personal brand and opens doors to new opportunities and collaborations. Johanna Reboullet highlighted how simple initiatives like researching guest speakers and sending thank-you messages can significantly enhance professional relationships and personal branding.

5. **Continuous Personal Growth and Adaptability:**

    Commit to lifelong learning and continuous improvement by pursuing ongoing education, certifications, and skill development. Demonstrating a commitment to lifelong learning enhances your expertise and keeps your personal brand relevant and competitive. Additionally, take responsibility for your actions and remain open to feedback. Use constructive criticism to refine and adapt your personal brand, ensuring it evolves with your goals and the world. Continuous improvement of ourselves and adaptability signal dedication to excellence to sustain long-term success. My dear former student Chloe Brendlinger often refers to this as "conscious marketing of oneself."

6. **Proactively Seizing or Creating Opportunities:** Stay vigilant and proactive in identifying and capitalizing on opportunities that align with your strengths and personal brand. Whether through networking events, industry trends, or unexpected encounters, maintain an open and curious mindset; it will enable you to create opportunities by launching side projects, starting businesses, or pursuing passions that demonstrate initiative and commitment.

7. **Accountability, Adaptability, and Resilience:** Take responsibility for your actions and decisions and remain open to feedback. Use constructive criticism to refine and adapt your personal brand, ensuring it also evolves over time. Accountability and adaptability help maintain a positive reputation and sustain long-term success. This includes recognizing the importance of delicate feedback delivery and how it affects others' perceptions of you, as highlighted by your personal experiences and student reflections. When our students share feedback with hospitality businesses, we do so with the utmost respect and care, to ensure we also leave that door open for future opportunities.

By the way, these tips do not mean I discourage folks from posting or sharing personal viewpoints—not at all. However, I would advise thinking twice before clicking "send email" or "post" because if opinions inadvertently and unexpectedly offend others, there's a potential consequence. It would be great if it could lead to open conversations and understanding, but the wild west of social media and discourse does not lean that way. Think before you post, as you consider your personal and professional brand.

My Brand? Tough Love.

One spring semester, I was showing a video of Morgan Spurlock's TED talk in which he interviewed everyday people and asked them, "What is your brand?" There were loads of hysterically funny responses:

"I'm eighties revival meets skater punk—unless it's laundry day."

"I'm dark glamor with sunglasses."

"If Dan were a car, he'd be a classic convertible Mercedes-Benz."

"Casual fly."

"I'm part hippie, part yogi, part Brooklyn girl."

"I'm the pet guy."

"Failed writer, alcoholic."

"I'm a lawyer brand."

My favorite is "My brand is FedEx—because I deliver the goods."

The last person questioned answered easily and smartly, "I'm Tom."

I then asked the students to take a few minutes to articulate their brand. And then something unusual happened. One student, one semester, suddenly raised her hand and asked, "Professor Lanz, what's your brand?" I was stumped because I didn't expect the question. No one had ever asked me that before. Suddenly, I responded rather easily. "Tough love.[6] My brand is tough love." And the class nodded in agreement, and we went on with the lesson.

Burning Bridges: Try Not To

Cultivating a personal brand with intention is paramount in the tightly knit global hospitality industry, where connections are often just two degrees apart. It's not about falsely representing ourselves, but about awareness and marketing oneself thoughtfully, carefully, and deliberately. This approach enhances professional reputation and fosters meaningful relationships within this expansive yet interconnected network.

While it's inevitable that not everyone will align harmoniously and disagreements sometimes impact our well-being (I've been there), maintaining decorum and presenting ourselves with pride remains essential. As we advance in our careers, we must distance ourselves from toxic influences, safeguarding our authentic selves. Embracing self-awareness and being open to constructive feedback can be challenging, yet these practices are crucial for personal growth.

It's not easy to completely avoid burning bridges. That's why I say, "try not to." We also want, as individuals, to be heard and respected in a manner that sometimes may offend or burn bridges. And I know I haven't always performed or "behaved" in a manner consistent with what I'm sharing here. Though I try, and I'm aware. I'm human, and I have opinions. But I'm also more seasoned in my experiences, and so yes, there's a bit of "I can say this now; I've seen things." As someone who still wants to contribute much more to my industry, I am aware of being careful and smart about my brand. Consistently delivering excellence in our work and remaining connected (marketing ourselves) builds trust and reliability, paving the way for unexpected opportunities, career advancements, and lifelong authentic relationships and friendships.

Moreover, it's not just Denise Dupre, my thesis advisor from the 1980s, who reappeared in my world in the 2020s as an advisory board member of the school where I work, but also others I've collaborated with throughout my career. Many are now in new roles, and our paths continue to cross, exemplifying the enduring connections and serendipitous encounters that make working in hospitality so rewarding. This ongoing network is a testament to the joy of building and maintaining meaningful relationships in the industry and delivering excellent work.

Marketing Mantras

In our globally networked environment, marketing oneself transcends the traditional promotion of products or services; it involves a mindful approach to how we present and engage with others to consciously market ourselves. Respecting people's time and genuinely listening to their needs fosters trust and meaningful connections. A simple "thank you" can leave a lasting impression, as individuals remember *how you made them feel*. By consistently connecting and building authentic relationships, we naturally market ourselves, creating a strong and supportive network that opens doors to new opportunities. Embracing these principles not only enhances our personal brand but also cultivates lasting bonds that are essential for both personal and professional growth.

1. **Integrate Personal and Professional Identities:**
   Recognize how our personal and professional identities influence one another.

2. **Demonstrate Authenticity with Respect:**
   Reflect authenticity in our actions and communications while respecting others' perspectives and values.

3. **Curate Digital Profiles Strategically:**
   Shape our digital profiles to reflect our brand values and support our professional goals, so they consistently represent who we are and what we stand for.

4. **Prioritize Meaningful Networking:**
   Engage intentionally in networking and relationship-building yet focus on creating genuine connections.

5. **Commit to Lifelong Learning:**
   Actively seek opportunities for personal and professional growth to expand our skills and knowledge.

By thoughtfully building and nurturing your personal brand, you set the stage for sustained success. Next, we will discuss the need to stay informed, remain relevant, and maintain strong connections to ensure your brand thrives in this non-stop, high-speed world we live in.

Mindset in Motion

As you embark on the personal branding journey, consider the unique identity you wish to cultivate professionally. Reflect on your story. What experiences have shaped who you are today? How can you consciously market yourself in a way that authentically represents your values and aspirations? Now think about the relationships you've built. Are there bridges you might need to reinforce instead of burn? As you craft your personal brand, ask yourself: What key messages do you want to convey? How will your brand resonate with others in your industry?

8

Stay Current, Relevant, and Connected

Whether you aim to run your own business or engage with various aspects of marketing in your career, familiarity with language, vocabulary, and systems empowers you to ask the right questions and contribute effectively to strategic decisions. By committing to continuous learning and keeping informed, you ensure that when you're involved in important decision-making, you can do so with intelligence and confidence regardless of your field.

Enough to be Dangerous

Staying up to date and connected is vital in any field or related discipline you choose to pursue. As I've shared earlier, in my digital marketing class, for example, I emphasize the mantra, "It's important to know enough to be dangerous," underscoring the value of having a foundational understanding even if you don't plan to specialize in digital marketing.

REACH[7] founder Dylan Huey shared with me for the *Boston Hospitality Review* how he obtains his news and what he considers reliable sources of information:

> In today's digital age, the abundance of information sources presents both an opportunity and a challenge. It's vital to sift through the noise to find trustworthy, reliable news. My approach involves a combination of news platforms, such as LinkedIn and YouTube, which offer a wide variety of perspectives and subscription services, such as Apple News, which aggregates content from leading global news providers.

> This hybrid approach allows me to stay up to date on industry trends, global events, and niche interests with information that is both timely and credible. The rise of social media as a primary news source reflects a general shift in consumption habits. Platforms like TikTok and Instagram have democratized news distribution, making it more accessible and raising questions about accuracy and bias. Navigating this

landscape requires a critical eye and a commitment to cross-referencing information, ensuring that one's understanding of the world is broad and correct.

It's important to read and continually learn; in this way, you can hold your own and "know enough to be dangerous." We need to know enough to ask the right questions. Know enough to contribute to the conversation. Yet, I also share my healthy reminder to always fact-check information and sources of information because, thanks to UGC (user-generated content), what I call "civilian journalism," and biased media, so much clutter of content is easily retrieved as accurate and factual. We should always verify sources. Please, verify all sources.

Recollections and Reflections

"'Know enough to be dangerous.' As our industry keeps evolving, it's important to stay curious and keep learning, as well as surround yourself with knowledgeable people. A few years after hearing this phrase in class, I also heard it at a business conference, reminding me of the valuable lesson and motivating me to keep growing and improving."

—Mai S., BU School of Hospitality,
Class of 2022 and MMH 2022

"Trends are evolving at such a fast pace. Reading is essential to keep up and prepare for whatever comes next. How can you help a brand in its marketing strategy if you haven't kept updated on what is happening around the world? In class, we worked with the boutique hotel, Maison Elle Paris, and assessed its social media strategy. Our help wouldn't have been relevant if we hadn't spent time reading about the features and nuances of each social media platform. It helped us understand that not all target markets use the same platform, naturally, and we adapt our social media campaign accordingly. For instance, we recommended that Maison Elle create a TikTok account to showcase their products and post videos of their events to attract more associates, which we classified as 'employer branding.' Even though TikTok is a globally recognized medium, I've never used it personally. Because we learned about its updates and usage, we really understood how important it is, especially for this client.

"Staying updated is also accomplished through your business contacts and relationships. I began to follow one of our class speakers, Virginie Le Norgant, co-CEO of GroupExpression in Paris. She often posts updates on her brand's partnerships and clients. It's an amazing way to discover new destinations and hotels that I have never heard of before. Connect to people and read what they share. It helps you stay relevant while building your personal brand."

—Johanna Reboullet,
ESSEC IMHI, Class of 2024

"Reflecting on our strategic marketing projects, the concept of 'stay current, stay relevant, stay connected' has been crucial to how I approach STAYCOOL. Back then, we learned that marketing isn't just about following trends but anticipating them. Today, this lesson drives everything we do at STAYCOOL, from staying on top of the latest style and social media trends to ensuring our messaging resonates with the culture of the moment. Staying connected with our audience is key; we constantly engage with our community online, listening to feedback and adapting in real time. That mindset started in our class and continues to shape our brand."

—Amin Adjmi,
BU School of Hospitality, Class of 2018

Adam Wallace, founder and CEO of New York City-based hospitality digital marketing agency Spherical, who has hired several of our digital marketing graduates over the years, also shared with me for the *Boston Hospitality Review*:

If you are a young marketer with an interest in hospitality, I recommend strongly leaning in to become a generalist. Great marketing requires interdisciplinary thinking in the interest of being creative and analytical. It's super helpful to understand all the elements and channels that influence someone's hotel (or any product) purchasing decision. It's key to be "versed in each—digital, social, advertising, email marketing, websites, analytics, revenue management, and sales.

As a marketer and in hospitality, keep an eye on consumer and media trends as you produce effective and creative marketing initiatives. By capitalizing on trends, you identify how to bring your client into that conversation and work magic for marketing. Read about related industries, too. Explore and have your own experiences and note what worked or didn't. Look at how restaurants personalize their experiences through menus or events. Look at the airline industry or cruise industry for messaging and how they speak to prospective guests. Consider the spa and wellness sector or destination marketing, and see how ads might resonate with you and your family or with colleagues.

Relationships: Make the Effort

Maintaining strong relationships is essential. Staying in touch ensures that your connections are robust and trustworthy. Here's a simple but important example. Important, because it changed chapters of my life: Terry Botten was the director of sales and marketing at the (then) new Four Seasons Hotel on the Boston Common in 1986. He saw my work when I was his intern, and we actively stayed in touch after my internship concluded. Years later, when he was with ITT Sheraton Hotels, the trust he had in me brought me to New York City with Sheraton. The quality of my work at Sheraton led many of my former colleagues, who had moved on to other positions in hospitality, to hire me for various projects years later when I was with HVS. This progression reinforces the importance of keeping up the hard work, gaining trust, and keeping in touch. By consistently nurturing these relationships, we create a network that supports ongoing collaboration and opens doors to new and wonderfully interesting, challenging, and meaningful opportunities.

In my classes today, and as mentioned earlier, I prioritize inclusive language by using "we" instead of "I" or "you." This subtle shift communicates to clients that we are all part of the same team, fostering a sense of unity and shared purpose. Saying "we" emphasizes that we are collectively working toward common goals, rather than operating as individuals or directing others. This approach is a crucial aspect of "staying connected" as it literally conveys that we are together and supportive of one another. It reinforces the idea that our success is a team effort, strengthening our internal and external relationships.

Employer branding is a pivotal strategy in attracting and retaining top talent. It involves marketing our businesses as great places to work, sometimes by encouraging employees to connect with potential future employees. This isn't just about outward appearances; it's about committing to our employees' well-being and professional development. With authentic care of employees and leveraging our existing workforce to build these connections, we enhance our reputation and make it easier to attract individuals who are aligned with our vision.

This is the value of great relationships. And they must be authentic, please.

Building and nurturing community relationships is another key aspect in this discussion. For example, as our class emphasized with Union Square Donuts – collaborations with local businesses and partnerships with Brookline community leaders or institutions, demonstrate our desire to engage productively within neighborhoods. Hotels (and other establishments, such as gyms or libraries) can position themselves as the center of community activities, fostering a sense of belonging and mutual support. These local engagements boost visibility and shows a dedication to positively supporting the areas we serve. We have the responsibility to contribute to the well-being of our community.

Read. Listen. Network.

What are some of the ways to stay relevant? Read. Listen. Network. Then read, listen, and network some more:

1. **Read Widely:**
   Receive the latest insights by subscribing to reputable industry-specific journals, newsletters, and online publications such as *Harvard Business Review*, *Ad Age*, and *Marketing Week*. Incorporate a mix of books, magazines, and online articles from various industries to gain broader perspectives and innovative ideas.

2. **Listen Actively:**

   Choose podcasts that feature industry leaders, case studies, and trend analyses like *Marketing Made Simple* and *Social Media Marketing Podcast*. Attend webinars and virtual conferences; participate in live webinars and virtual events to hear directly from experts and engage in real-time discussions.

3. **Engage Visually:**

   Follow influential YouTube channels and webinars, and subscribe to channels such as HubSpot. Listen to TED talks for tutorials, trend analyses, and expert interviews. Regularly review infographics and visual data reports to grasp complex information and trends quickly. Remember to verify your sources for legitimacy.

4. **Participate in Professional Networks:**

   Join the American Marketing Association (AMA) or, of course, HSMAI, the Hospitality Sales and Marketing Association International, and your local professional chapter. Join other local business groups. Engage in LinkedIn groups and Reddit forums where professionals discuss the latest trends and share valuable resources.

5. **Leverage Technology for Information Management:**

   Use RSS Feeds and aggregators such as Feedly to consolidate updates from multiple sources into one convenient platform. Set Google Alerts for key topics, competitors, and industry terms to receive timely updates directly into your inbox.

6. **Attend Conferences and Networking Events:**

Attend in-person or virtual conferences to hear from thought leaders, discover new technologies, and network with peers. Regularly attend local business meetups, seminars, and workshops to build connections and stay informed about regional trends.

7. **Collaborate and Share Knowledge:**

Discuss trends and insights with colleagues and peers to exchange knowledge and ideas. Share and reflect through blog posts, presentations, or panel discussions to reinforce your understanding and contribute to the community.

And Read Some More

I encourage students to read, watch, view, participate in, and apply insights to the marketing objectives desired. Encouraging students to read is one of my dominant philosophies. Read magazines that have nothing to do with the marketing subject matter to identify best practices from other industries. Watch brand messaging and analyze along the way. Don't simply let the message glance you by, but take note of the words used, the script, the imagery, the color, and the story shared in an ad, commercial, or YouTube video. I'm a fan of using the right words to get the message across in a nuanced and meaningful way.

The books I assign are easy reads and intended to help influence a marketing mindset. I find reading a book of practical examples with life lessons much more enjoyable than a textbook without real-world application.

> "One of my favorite memories of our class is that we did not read textbooks. We read practical books that shared real examples. They were relatable with recent and relevant cases for us to learn from. The books we used simplified the theories and principles we needed to know with real-world applications."
>
> —Kim Kibler, BS Boston University SHA 2018

The books I've included in my classes, for example, are:

1. *The Conscious Marketer* by (my college classmate) Jim Joseph: This collection of personal yet professional blog posts presents digestible chapters that quickly get to its point: All marketing should include some element of corporate social responsibility (CSR). As my students know, in previous years, all our marketing projects needed to include a recommendation for CSR. Today, all our marketing challenges need to incorporate community engagement, wellness, or sustainability as integral and authentic messaging for our hospitality businesses.

2. *Talk Like TED* by Carmine Gallo: Gallo is such a great writer, and this in-depth analysis of what constitutes a successful TED talk is clearly

structured into nine easy-to-follow steps. I read the first three chapters of this book every August while enjoying a summer day on the beach in Westhampton, so I can refresh and prepare for the semesters ahead. I ask the students to read this book so they understand a few concepts as they prepare for their final marketing presentations. For example, Gallo shares that TED talks are limited to eighteen minutes, aligning with research on attention spans. Gallo cited TED curator Chris Anderson's reasoning of the time limit as "short enough to hold people's attention, including on the Internet, and precise enough to be taken seriously."

3. *Start with Why* by Simon Sinek: I also show Sinek's *Start with Why* TED video in class. The video emphasizes Simon's concept of the "Golden Circle," which consists of three concentric circles: "why," "how," and "what." Sinek suggests that too many organizations and leaders focus primarily on what they offer, rather than why, which is the deeper sense of purpose, as we alluded to earlier. Marketers need to understand why they need to connect with target audiences in a more personalized manner.

We've had a variety of marketing case studies and articles that have also been used in our marketing courses. I tend to use contemporary press or magazine articles to incorporate relatable issues into the course and to help infuse the need to keep up with news. For example, there's a *Long Island Newsday* article about Northwell Healthcare's far-too-long and expensive rebranding and repositioning effort. I encourage students to also review additional related articles and YouTube videos, which include the television commercials that were developed to launch Northwell's (then) new name and brand.

Additionally, articles about food influencers and how they can make or break a restaurant's business, or articles about the communication (or lack of communication) of Starbucks' and Dunkin's changes to their loyalty programs, are also among our readings, which are updated periodically, so we always assess contemporary and relatable scenarios.

Student Memory

Celina was a standout student in three of my undergraduate classes; it's as if she "majored in Professor Lanz." We continue to stay connected, occasionally exchanging insights. I've had the pleasure of watching her evolve from a dedicated college student into a successful professional with a strong marketing mindset. Here she shares a fond memory of a lesson learned from one of our class experiences:

"I took several of our marketing classes, overlapping with two Super Bowls. One might ask, 'Why is there an entire class session dedicated to a football game on a university marketing syllabus?' The answer was clear: a seemingly mere thirty-second advertising slot for the price of $6 to $7 million. Following the big game, my classmates and I strolled into class, opened our notebooks to pages with headers like 'initial reactions,' and spent the entire lecture analyzing the most buzzworthy commercials.

"Super Bowl commercials are a staple of American culture. These commercials transcend traditional marketing as Americans sit back like judges on American Idol, ready to give the thumbs up or thumbs down to our beloved brands and bold newcomers. As marketing students and millennials, we looked to see if corporate America had a pulse on the general populace. When I invited Sam Schweikert, the star of Anheuser-Busch's 2017 'Born the Hard Way' commercial, to speak to our marketing class, I learned that filming took place at least seven months before game day. A lot can change in that time. The stakes are high in a world of cancel culture and brand boycotts.

"Once the game is called and the confetti has long been swept off the field, these micro-moments of entertainment live on through YouTube and other forms of content sharing (racking millions of views and reactions). Whether it's a familiar celebrity face or outrageous uses of special effects that evoke surprise or humor, we cannot deny the cultural impact that can be leveraged.

"While there are many formulas for success, there are key lessons to learn from studying Super Bowl ads: *Stay relevant by staying on brand. Stay relevant through the art of storytelling. And stay relevant by creating content that is shareable.*

"This is accomplished when a brand knows its audience and creates ads that resonate with them to provide value. Sam's Super Bowl commercial with Anheuser-Busch showcases a history of tradition built into the brand's identity. While nothing in the ad had anything to do with beer itself, the majestic Clydesdale horses are forever synonymous with Anheuser-Busch's Budweiser. Fans tune in every year to watch the famous horses cinematically shine. People remember ads that evoke conversation and strong emotion. Not every brand needs a commercial that makes you want to reach for the tissue box, but it sure can make Uncle Mike belly laugh until Sprite is coming out of his nose. The whole family will be laughing about it until the Fourth of July."

—Celina Friedman,
BU School of Hospitality, Class of 2016

Marketing Mantras

1. **Cultivate and Maintain Relationships:**
   As illustrated by Terry Botten's support of my work when transitioning from Four Seasons to Sheraton, consistent engagement and trust can lead to invaluable opportunities. By prioritizing relationship-building, you create a reliable network that not only supports your present

endeavors but also opens doors to future collaborations and career advancements.

2. **Embrace Inclusive Language to Foster Team Unity:**

    Using "we" instead of "I" or "you" is more than just a linguistic choice; it signifies a collective effort and shared responsibility. This subtle shift in communication reinforces the idea that everyone is part of the same team, working toward common goals.

3. **Invest Time and Effort in Employer Branding:**

    Effective employer branding is essential for attracting and retaining top talent. By marketing your organization as a great place to work and encouraging employees to connect with potential hires, you build a strong reputation that aligns with your values and vision. Additionally, actively engaging with the community through partnerships with local businesses and influencers enhances visibility, demonstrates a commitment to the areas served, and positions you as a trusted and integral part of the community.

By diligently staying informed, remaining relevant, and fostering meaningful connections, we equip ourselves to make smarter, more impactful decisions and confidently seize emerging opportunities. By applying critical thinking, honing strategic approaches, and even mastering the art of marketing oneself, we can better navigate the challenges and opportunities that lie ahead.

Mindset in Motion

Staying current and relevant is essential for success. Reflect on your efforts to keep your knowledge fresh. What strategies have you implemented to ensure you are always learning and growing? Consider the relationships you've cultivated. How can you deepen these connections to expand your network and gain new insights? As you read, listen, and engage with your community, think about the new ideas and perspectives you can bring into your professional journey. Ask yourself, "What steps will I take to stay connected and continuously evolve in my field?"

The Marketing Mindset Scorecard

Marketing Yourself

Chapters 7 and 8

Milestone: From Passive Presence to Personal Brand Advocate

Concept	1 (Needs Work)	3 (Getting There)	5 (Fully Integrated)
Personal Branding	I don't actively manage my professional image	I have an online presence, but don't optimize it or keep it fresh	I consciously build and refine my professional brand
Staying Current and Connected	I rarely engage with marketing trends or network	I follow trends but don't engage in conversations	I read, network, and contribute thought leadership

Reflection Questions:

- Are you consciously shaping your professional brand or leaving it to chance?
- How often do you invest in learning new marketing trends and skills?

PART III

What Does the Future Hold?

CHAPTER 9

Marketing for the Future: Innovation, Sustainability, and Social Impact

Today, corporate social responsibility (CSR) is still a widely recognized term, but *social impact* has become a more modern and preferred way to describe a company's contributions to society. The shift in terminology reflects a broader, more action-oriented approach to sustainability, ethics, and community engagement.

Many companies now use social impact, ESG (environmental, social, and governance), or purpose-driven business to signal a deeper integration of responsibility into their core strategy rather than a separate initiative.

CSR is sometimes seen as an older, compliance-driven concept, while *social impact* suggests proactive, measurable, and systemic change.

That said, CSR is still in use, especially in traditional industries and regions where it has long been established. The choice between CSR and social impact often depends on the company's branding, audience, and strategic focus.

> There are at least four essential pillars that the hospitality industry is uniquely positioned to address: innovation, sustainability, wellness, and community engagement—the latter of which intersects meaningfully with all three. These areas collectively redefine how we create, communicate, and deliver exceptional customer experiences.

Innovation encompasses creative offerings and novel marketing strategies that enhance and elevate our connections with employees and guests. Sustainability emerges as a fundamental responsibility, where the convergence of hospitality and environmental stewardship affirms our duty to protect people, places, and the planet. And an emphasis on wellness highlights the importance of providing personalized and memorable experiences that nurture the holistic well-being of our employees and guests. Community engagement reinforces each of these pillars by fostering meaningful connections with local partners, giving voice to stakeholders, and ensuring that (hospitality) experiences are rooted in relevance, inclusion, and shared value.

I want to encourage marketers and service professionals across lodging, restaurants, tourism, hospitality-adjacent related sectors (senior living and residential housing), and other service businesses to prioritize responsibility and deliver meaningful, positive impact. In this way, hospitality can continue to thrive while fostering genuine connections and enhancing quality of life.

Rationale

The selection of these topics is very personal for me as an experienced hospitality marketer and as a human. These four areas are crucial for shaping effective marketing strategies. They address modern travelers' immediate needs and preferences while aligning with broader societal trends and values, making them essential areas of concentration for marketers aiming to stay relevant, competitive, and principled. I also strongly believe that:

> If hospitality is about how we make
> people feel, don't we have a responsibility
> to authentically connect with people,
> showing that we genuinely care
> about their well-being and the overall
> sustainability of people, place, and planet?

Innovation drives continuous improvement and differentiation. In an era where technology evolves rapidly and customer expectations constantly shift, approaches such as artificial intelligence and virtual reality in service or reimagined service delivery and operational processes are vital for enhancing guest experiences and efficiency.

Sustainability is essential. Consumers and stakeholders demand that businesses operate responsibly and contribute positively to the planet and communities. Marketing authentic sustainability initiatives communicates a brand's commitment to ethical practices, attracting a growing segment of environmentally aware consumers (as long as we are not greenwashing.

Wellness has become a central focus in hospitality as travelers desire holistic experiences that promote their physical, mental, and emotional well-being. Marketing wellness initiatives and amenities position hospitality brands as facilitators of comprehensive and enriching guest experiences (so long as we are not "wellness-washing").

Together, these priorities — when supported by genuine **community engagement** — enable (hospitality) brands to create experiences that are innovative, responsible, and wellness-driven, while deeply rooted in local relevance and shared values.

Innovation–Technological or Otherwise

Fresh thinking in administrative processes and service delivery is just as transformative as technological measures for the hospitality industry. By reimagining and streamlining our operational procedures, we can allow our teams to dedicate more time to connecting with guests and customers on a meaningful level, elevating the overall guest experience.

Below, I share a selection of projects and insights from the professionals and alums who have contributed to our classroom learning over the years. These examples illustrate our commitment to staying ahead of trends and fostering a forward-thinking mindset for emerging marketers. I aim to align our classroom marketing recommendations with contemporary issues and inspire continual innovation, ensuring our approach remains fresh and responsive to the dynamic demands of the market.

Recollections and Reflections

Adaptability to Improve with Technological Capabilities: "Adaptability and continuous learning are crucial. We must stay attuned to the evolving landscape and pivot when necessary. This flexibility is key to long-term success in both marketing and personal branding. I'm particularly confident in adapting to changes driven by AI advancements. In my freelance web design, branding, and marketing business, I've seen how AI tools enhance both the creative and technical sides of the design process. We must embrace technological changes that are shaping our industries, whether we like them or not. Growing with these changes, rather than resisting them, is essential."

—Corinne Ognibene,
BU School of Hospitality, Class of 2017

Streamlining Processes for Customer Convenience: "In my role as a property and operations manager (for residential buildings), I see the parallels and needs for hospitality. In addition to target marketing, another marketing lesson I clearly recall involves the use of artificial intelligence. How do we improve technologies while retaining humanity and hospitality? So, let's take the renovation of a building lobby for example. The building now utilizes a virtual doorman intercom system for front door entry. We equipped the lobby with an Amazon Hub Locker to retrieve packages at the concierge desk. Tenants can access their packages twenty-four hours a day, seven days a week, using the Amazon app. AI is vital in the future of hospitality; it's streamlining processes. The more efficient the innovation and technology to meet the customer needs and wants, the more we know we are marketing better."

—Josh Ohebshalom,
BU School of Hospitality, Class of 2020

Use Contemporary Amenities as Customer Solutions: "Think about your marketing messages. For example, let's consider electric charging stations. The hotel likely installed them as a convenience and potential revenue generator. But market them! It's your unique selling proposition, and you are connecting and satisfying the needs of and providing a solution for drivers of electric vehicles. Remember to communicate the amenities you have to resonate with the audiences who will appreciate them."

—Marut K. Raval,
BU School of Hospitality, Class of 2020, MMH 2021

Customer Data Platforms to Enable Customer Preferences: In the May edition of the *Boston Hospitality Review*, another fellow Long Islander and hospitality marketer, my colleague Roger Drake (formerly interim CMO at Condado Tacos), explained:

> Technology implementation for existing and new guests has ongoing benefits for Condado's marketing efforts. Hospitality means knowing who your guests are, where they come from, and their dining preferences to the extent that it doesn't feel too "big brother" and obtrusive. There is continued utilization of advanced technology, such as smart devices for order taking and back-of-house reduction in overall ticket times, without sacrificing human interaction with guests. The more knowledge we can ascertain about the brand's loyal guests and newly acquired guests, the better.
>
> It's also important for Condado to identify the guest journey, for example, other lifestyle brands they prefer

and other retailers along "the guest path" that complement the dining preferences. This helps create a comprehensive guest profile, thereby establishing a better familiarity and recognition that they have earned status as a "regular."

AI in Architecture and Design: Spherical CEO Adam Wallace is someone whose firm I've admired from afar for many years now. His creative digital marketing agency represents and works internationally with some of the most incredible properties. Adam grew up in the hotel business, and staying relevant to hospitality is key for him. When we chatted for our school's *Boston Hospitality Review,* he shared:

> I like what I'm seeing in AI applications in architecture and interior design. The speed of creative application and innovation is tremendous. Designers can go from written prompts to full visualizations immediately. I don't think this will limit the need for designers and architects; rather, it will push creative thinking further and faster.

> Much of hotel technology has been behind in innovation, still stuck on figuring out relatively fundamental tech systems. I do think, however, that we are closer to all systems speaking to each other more seamlessly, which will unlock the opportunity for hoteliers to deliver a much more personalized experience to guests, both digitally and on property.

Reimagining Engagement with Innovative Marketing

Virtual Reality for Immersive Experiences: In the Fall 2017 semester, one of our key marketing challenges involved partnering with Turkish Airlines as the company added routes into Boston. During this period, the Istanbul airport terminal underwent significant renovation and expansion to accommodate the growing passenger traffic. We aimed to market the new Boston service as a more affordable alternative for travelers heading to various European destinations, including Turkey. We also sought to encourage passengers using the newly upgraded Istanbul terminal to explore the enhanced facilities and the historic city itself. To achieve this, our students proposed the innovative use of virtual reality headsets in the airport lounges. These VR oculars would showcase Istanbul's iconic attractions and rich cultural heritage, offering travelers a virtual taste of the ancient city and enticing them to immerse themselves in the destination during their layover or onward journey.

I also recall visiting the MGM Grand in Las Vegas with my family (decades ago), where arcade-style games and virtual or augmented reality activities provided engaging entertainment for all ages. Similarly, incorporating such interactive experiences within airport lounges can significantly enhance passenger engagement and satisfaction. We can create moments that resonate with customers by offering activities that keep travelers active and entertained while remaining indoors. These engaging interactions also encourage powerful word-of-mouth marketing, as guests, diners, and passengers share their positive experiences with others.

My former teaching assistant Kim Kibler and I discussed other "innovative platforms" which have become more mainstream. Is your brand utilizing Spotify, perhaps, to compose a branded song list (as we recommended for a health club in Boston's North End, for example)? Is your voice a part of the conversation on Alexa when someone asks a question? If not, someone else's voice will be there first.

These innovations represent just the tiny tip of the mammoth iceberg when it comes to reimagining engagement and entertainment in hospitality marketing, and are just smaller classroom samplings to whet the marketing-mindset appetite. As technology continues to evolve, opportunities for creativity and connection expand exponentially. Beyond technology, innovations in storytelling, like branded podcasts or gamified experiences, allow brands to connect with audiences on a deeper, personal level. The challenge—and the opportunity—is to embrace a mindset of curiosity and experimentation to connect, pushing the boundaries of what's possible and inspiring loyalty and trust in entirely new ways.

Sustainability

After two consecutive summers of vacation travel adversely impacted by climate change, my view on incorporating sustainability into the thread of hospitality marketing became emphatic. I strongly believe that all businesses are responsible for doing the right thing and contributing to the good of the community and the betterment of their location while ensuring the protection of the environment and the planet.

So, in the fall semester of 2023, I shifted my marketing course with a renewed emphasis on social responsibility, integrating sustainability as a central theme. I spoke with Boston-area hospitality businesses to participate in the Experiential Marketing class, allowing students to conduct due diligence and make reasonable recommendations for implementing environmentally friendly initiatives that result in a return on investment for the owners. The students responded to these projects with notable enthusiasm. This is an important issue for this generation of travelers and the future workforce.

> Wellness is that of an individual's mind, body, spirit, and soul.
> Sustainability is the wellness of people, place, and the planet.

Classroom Cases

Our projects were, as expected, challenging. For instance, an iconic 300-year-old Boston food hall, attraction, and landmark was certainly not built by the Bostonians of colonial times to be environmentally sound or recycling-forward. Similarly, a local hotel offered several environmentally friendly features but did not qualify as a truly "green" hotel. During this process, we educated the management and ownership about the concept of "greenwashing" and the importance of achieving criteria set by The American Hotel and Lodging Association's Green Key designation and Booking.com's sustainability "leaves." Understanding these certifications helped our partners recognize the tangible benefits of authentic sustainability efforts. A key challenge involved positioning Boston as appealing to both locals and visitors by developing community-focused experiences marketed through hotel concierge itineraries, and collaborating with a broad coalition of Greater Boston tourism advocates to communicate our sustainability goals.

Throughout that semester, we learned that sustainability must be proactively marketed. Promoting a business's sustainability efforts is not exploitative; it is essential. Consumers increasingly seek companies with shared values, particularly pertaining to environmental responsibility. Businesses that fail to communicate their sustainability initiatives risk losing customers to competitors who do. And, of course, it's essential to avoid overstating sustainability efforts—(as previously mentioned), commonly known as "greenwashing." Today's consumers aren't looking for a hard sell; they value honest communication, education, and an ongoing relationship with the brand.

Our hospitality projects were challenging, and please remember that our students' recommendations were based on analyzing the situation, conducting primary and secondary research, including a competitive analysis and digital footprint assessment, determining target markets, and developing an overall campaign. Here's a glimpse at some of the real-world sustainability marketing challenges our students were asked to solve:

- *How do we recommend marketing solutions for a conservation and wildlife-focused attraction that already has a powerful marketing machine?* The Franklin Park Zoo is an institution with a strong mission of conservation, yet our task was to suggest enhancements to their current marketing strategies. That's not easy when the organization already has a strong marketing machine. Our students recommended education at various visitor touchpoints to further enhance the zoo experience. Education and communication of the environmental information are critical to mobilizing the brand and connecting with guests.

- *What sustainability initiatives can we recommend for a US historic attraction that is exempt from local environmental guidelines, and how do we encourage stakeholders to buy in?* Faneuil Hall Marketplace was not designed with modern recycling or sustainability expectations in mind. It also encompasses numerous vendors who need to understand the importance of recycling and sustainability needs. Among its many recommendations, the team suggested an internal communications plan to teach the food hall vendors about the initiatives needed to remain competitive among today's traveling population and developed a "badge" system to motivate the vendors to participate and market their evolving sustainability and food-waste initiatives.

- *How do we communicate to a hotel that its claims of "green" and "eco-friendly" would require more initiatives to avoid greenwashing?* The Marriott Courtyard Hotel in Cambridge, Massachusetts, considered itself "sustainable" and "green." The students were eager to understand the level of commitment to determine if more initiatives were needed for authentic marketing opportunities. We researched the American Hotel and Lodging Association's criteria and the city of Boston's needs to meet expectations for the years 2030 and 2050, and we studied other hotels with sustainability claims throughout the United States. Hotels have much more to do than use refillable water bottles or put beehives on the roofs to use the word sustainability comfortably.

- *What activities can we recommend to a sustainability-focused shop to strengthen its community engagement and boost local awareness and support?* In 2023, Uvida was the sole zero-waste retail store in Boston (it's located in Brookline, Massachusetts), offering eco-friendly refill options for household items. It's a neighborhood favorite among eco-conscious residents, yet the store lacked its due awareness and visibility. The students strongly urged the young, female, entrepreneurial founder to share her stories through social media and create an event-marketing effort to invite locals and create community. The proprietor and creator of Uvida was only twenty-four at the time.

- *Is it exploitive to market our sustainability initiatives, or should we promote them? And if so, how?* Levy's Food Service at the Boston Convention and Exposition Center (BCEC) is noteworthy for its sustainability efforts, local food sourcing, and food donation programs. But it was resistant to marketing these efforts for fear of seeming boastful and exploitive. How can we tell them it's ok to educate their audiences? The students conducted in-depth research to discover that it is not only "ok" to market your practices; it's essential, and people are willing to spend more with your business if your business is "doing good." Students suggested updates to the website, social media, and on-site signage, and even proposed RFP copy to ensure the venue's impressive. environmentally friendly initiatives could be communicated across key touchpoints for both meeting planners and attendees.

- *What measures can we recommend to a large primary urban destination to create a mindset for sustainable living and tourism?* Meet Boston is the destination marketing organization dedicated to enhancing local communities, supporting hospitality businesses, and promoting tourism. The agency sought additional insight to help define and prioritize its sustainability narrative. The student team created a double-pronged approach to raise our "sustainability senses," as we will read below.

These projects highlighted the necessity of a thoughtful and honest approach to sustainability marketing and taught us the importance of promoting good deeds by transparently communicating their impact. Remember, sustainability initiatives must also make financial sense and align with ownership goals to achieve true success.

Case Studies

Here are deeper insights into two of the projects above, revealing the challenges and opportunities in building trust and inspiring action, while driving engagement among stakeholders.

Communicating Sustainability for Meet Boston: Boston offers something for everyone, from its revolutionary history and beloved sports teams to its world-class universities and vibrant arts scene. In recent years, Boston's twenty-three neighborhoods have emerged as leaders in sustainability, excelling in environmental programs, support for immigrant success, green spaces, LEED regulations, and alternative fuel stations. Additionally,

Boston is recognized for its diversity, as illustrated by the Boston Indicators' Diversity Index of 70 percent, indicating a high likelihood of racial and ethnic diversity among residents.

Recognizing the importance of effectively communicating these sustainability efforts, our students developed a comprehensive marketing plan for Meet Boston. By leveraging thorough research and industry collaboration, the students created a two-phased campaign targeting three key themes: people, place, and planet. The strategies aim to enhance awareness, foster a strong digital and physical presence, and promote sustainable practices among residents, travelers, and partners.

Challenges and Initiatives: The primary challenge was to instill a sense of responsibility in residents, travelers, and current Meet Boston members to adopt a sustainability-conscious mindset. As a globally recognized city, Boston has a significant platform to drive change, but effective communication of sustainability efforts is essential to maximize impact. Key challenges included:

1. **Awareness and Integration:**
   Ensuring both newcomers and established populations are integrated with mutual care and sustainability practices.

2. **Community Engagement:**

Encouraging participation in city-wide sustainability efforts and educating both travelers and locals on sustainable tourism.

3. **Preventing Greenwashing:**

Maintaining genuine sustainability practices without misleading stakeholders, thereby building trust and loyalty.

Strategic Solutions: The student team developed a strategic marketing plan focusing on three themes to address these challenges:

1. **People:**

Emphasizing social sustainability by ensuring the local community lives sustainably before promoting the city as a sustainable destination.

2. **Place:**

Promoting economic sustainability by driving tourism and business to Boston's underrepresented and unique areas.

3. **Planet:**

Highlighting environmental sustainability to ensure both tourists and locals contribute to leaving the city better off than they found it.

Recommendations: To effectively communicate Meet Boston's sustainability efforts, the students proposed developing targeted communication strategies to educate the target markets with its "Sustainably Yours, Boston" campaign, emphasizing each neighborhood's unique sustainability initiatives.

Communicating Sustainability for Levy's Food Service at the Boston Convention and Exposition Center: Levy's Food Service is the official food service provider for the Boston Convention and Exposition Center (BCEC). The commitment to enhancing sustainability at the BCEC began in 2006 when the Massachusetts Convention Center Authority (MCCA), in partnership with the Massachusetts Department of Environmental Protection (DEP) and the U.S. Environmental Protection Agency (EPA) New England, launched a comprehensive plan to redirect food waste through composting.

Challenges and Initiatives: The BCEC has made significant strides in advancing sustainability over the past decade. Collaborating with Save That Stuff, the MCCA successfully reduced recyclable waste by an average of 774 tons annually across the Hynes Convention Center and BCEC venues. In 2016, the BCEC achieved LEED Silver certification from the U.S. Green Building Council, underscoring its dedication to environmental responsibility, resource efficiency, and effective waste management. Additionally, the BCEC introduced the Signature Boston's Conventions C.A.R.E. Program in 2010, which has donated over 200 tons of goods to local nonprofit organizations.

In 2019, in collaboration with Levy Restaurants and Green City Growers, the BCEC established The Chef's Garden. This initiative has provided over 500 pounds of fresh produce to the homeless in Boston through Pine Street Inn, a nonprofit organization offering essential services, housing, and workforce development for homeless individuals.

Levy Restaurants, founded in 1978 as a delicatessen, has grown into a multinational catering, foodservice, and event management corporation. In 2006, Levy was acquired by Compass Group, making it the largest catering company in the United States. Since the acquisition, Levy has significantly reduced waste and promoted an environmentally sustainable image. A key component of these efforts was the creation of WasteNot (now WasteNot 2.0), Levy's comprehensive waste tracking and monitoring system used company-wide for ESG tracking and reporting.

Both Levy and the BCEC continue to advance sustainability practices internally (employee-facing) and externally (guest-facing). This case study aims to recommend strategies for effectively communicating these efforts.

Strategic Solutions: Chef Kaeo Yuen has implemented impressive sustainability initiatives throughout the BCEC venue and its food service operations. However, a critical question remains: Are meeting planners, attendees, and the broader hospitality community aware of these efforts? While the initiatives are well-established internally, their communication to external stakeholders may not yet be fully developed.

Levy manages a foodservice operation that serves over 1.3 million guests annually, with current levels surpassing pre-pandemic numbers. Two primary issues were identified from Levy's perspective: first, a bottleneck in client communications, particularly regarding last-minute guest count changes, which impact their ability to operate sustainably; second, the challenge of effectively convincing meeting planners to incorporate more green initiatives into their events.

By conducting detailed primary and secondary research, identifying target markets and personas, and selecting effective delivery methods, the student team developed a series of research-backed recommendations to enhance communications and highlight the extensive sustainability efforts.

Recommendations: Ultimately, our communication-focused recommendations aim to integrate, encourage, and educate both internal and external constituents. The resulting marketing strategy includes a comprehensive communication plan with elements to:

- **Educate Internal Employees:**
  Implement training programs and informational sessions to ensure all staff are knowledgeable about sustainability initiatives.

- **Engage Conference Attendees:**
  Utilize in-building rotating signage and storytelling to showcase sustainability efforts and inspire attendees.
- **Communicate with Meeting Planners:**
  Develop targeted communication strategies to inform and persuade meeting planners to adopt more green practices in their events.

The overarching marketing theme, "Integrate, Encourage, Educate—Our Sustainability Story," seeks to effectively communicate Levy and BCEC's sustainability initiatives. By fostering greater awareness and engagement, Levy can strengthen its commitment to sustainability, enhance its reputation, and encourage customer loyalty.

Our main takeaways from both projects? If we have sustainable initiatives, it is crucial to actively market them. Consumers are increasingly willing to pay more for hotels, restaurants, and establishments that contribute positively to people, places, and the planet. Failing to promote our sustainability efforts can result in customers turning to competitors who are effectively communicating their initiatives.

Measuring Sustainability Success

Establishing clear metrics for evaluating sustainability helps organizations refine their strategies, maintain transparency, and build trust with consumers, employees, and investors. Here are some steps to "start with the end goals" for such initiatives:

1. **Define Key Performance Indicators (KPIs):**

   These metrics should align with a company's sustainability goals. Would your goals for improvement require environmental, social, or economic metrics?

   - Environmental Metrics track reductions in carbon emissions, energy consumption, or water usage.
   - Social Metrics measure diversity in hiring practices, employee engagement, or contributions to local communities.
   - Economic Metrics assess cost savings from sustainable operations or revenue generated through eco-friendly offerings.

   For example, a hotel implementing energy-efficient lighting might monitor monthly energy savings, while a restaurant sourcing locally could track the percentage of ingredients purchased from regional suppliers.

2. **Leverage Technology for Data Collection:**

   Tools like smart sensors, waste tracking systems, and customer data platforms can provide real-time insights into resource usage and efficiency. For example, Levy's WasteNot 2.0 system tracks food waste across operations, offering valuable data for reducing inefficiencies and enhancing sustainability. Similarly, hotels adopting smart energy systems can monitor and optimize energy consumption. These technologies simplify data and make it easier to share results with stakeholders.

3. **Evaluate Guest and Community Impact:**

   Sustainability isn't only about environmental metrics; it's also about the guest experience and community engagement. Surveys and feedback tools can help businesses measure how well their initiatives resonate with customers. We can conduct post-stay surveys asking guests how they perceive the hotel's eco-friendly practices, and engage locals and partners to assess the social and economic benefits of sustainability programs.

   For example, the Franklin Park Zoo's conservation messaging could be evaluated by analyzing visitor feedback on how the sustainability efforts influence their perception of the animal park's mission.

4. **Compare Against Industry Standards:**

   Recognitions like the Green Key Global certification or LEED ratings validate sustainability efforts and offer a framework for improvement. A hotel achieving Booking.com's sustainability "leaves" can use that as a benchmark to measure future progress.

5. **Communicate Results Effectively:**

   Transparency is key. Share both successes and areas for improvement. Storytelling can play a powerful role here, and we can use digital platforms or visuals to do so. For example, use websites and social media to highlight measurable impacts, such as the amount of waste diverted from landfills or carbon emissions reduced. Infographics and dashboards can translate complex data into more accessible and engaging formats for a broader audience.

   Levy's use of rotating signage within the Boston Convention and Exposition Center is an excellent example of how to communicate sustainability initiatives directly to guests in an impactful way.

6. **Link Sustainability to Financial Returns:**

   Cost savings from energy-efficient operations or increased customer loyalty due to eco-friendly practices can be quantified and shared. A lodging company can compare utility costs before and after implementing energy-efficient upgrades to demonstrate the financial viability of sustainable investments.

7. **Build a Culture of Accountability:**

   Regular audits, employee training, and stakeholder engagement ensure that sustainability remains a priority. Empowering employees to contribute ideas and participate in initiatives fosters a sense of ownership and accountability, driving continuous improvement.

Sustainability is not a one-time effort; it's a continuous commitment of innovation and transparency. Marketers can help companies demonstrate genuine leadership in sustainability, inspiring trust and loyalty among audiences.

Wellness

Wellness, like sustainability, became another personal issue I wanted to address in our marketing classes. Due to a severe illness of a loved one, I wanted to learn more about the intersection of wellness and hospitality. I once again relied on the knowledge of incredible friends to guide my fall 2024 class with clever insight.

Wellness, like hospitality, is about making people feel good, mentally and physically. Physical health boosts emotional health and vice versa. Our industry is responsible for ensuring wellness and sustainability are central to how we connect with people; this focus ultimately enriches the guest experience, the employees' offerings, and the owners' return.

Our class projects included luxury hotel spas, an independent, stand-alone spa, a cannabis dispensary, and a lifestyle hotel wanting to engage more in wellness.

Through our friend Kris Covarrubias of Boston University's Office of Student Wellbeing, we learned the definitions of the multi-dimensions of wellness:

- Social: Fostering meaningful connections
- Physical: Promoting movement and health
- Environmental: Creating harmonious surroundings
- Intellectual: Encouraging personal growth and learning
- Financial: Supporting economic well-being
- Spiritual: Nurturing inner peace and purpose
- Emotional: Building resilience and mental health

These pillars reflect a holistic framework for designing wellness encounters. Our class used these pillars to show how in-room hotel offerings, restaurant and room-service menu items, and other touchpoints of the guest experience, in hotels, independent spas, or elsewhere, are integral to offering personalized options for every individual. The students proposed creative initiatives, including an iPad or spa concierge to ask guests about their state of mind or physical condition and to recommend tailored, onsite spa services or local neighborhood activities. Other ideas featured menu items designed to fuel guests healthfully and initiatives that showed wellness can be fun and engaging, not just serious and intimidating.

Group activities that foster social connection and cultivate relationships—and even engage with the local community—can also add a meaningful perspective to wellness offerings, encouraging guests to step out of the hotel and participate in local activities.

Classroom Cases

Our student teams proposed brand-aligned partnerships to enhance offerings and reach broader audiences. For example, we suggested incorporating vibrant, health-focused juices to complement rooftop yoga classes at a lifestyle hotel known for its edgy and sassy appeal. Another idea involved organizing Gen-Z social events hosted by nationally recognized influencers at coastal beach hut locations, with proceeds supporting critical philanthropic causes supported by a lifestyle beverage that was positioned to complement active, balanced living and social celebration.

In one or two cases, collaborations with publications and entertainment activities geared to audiences with "higher or more demanding expectations" were suggested, broadening the reach of the marketing messaging. We encouraged our "clients" to prioritize education for their internal teams and guests, focusing on the deeper, more meaningful aspects of their offerings. Instead of promoting products, the marketing should inform wellness-seekers about how these services can positively impact their well-being and seamlessly integrate into their routines, moving beyond the idea of a one-time indulgence.

We learned about how biophilic design, incorporating natural elements into hospitality spaces, enhances guest well-being by fostering calm and reducing stress. Whether through green spaces, natural materials, or maximizing sunlight, this approach connects people to nature and aligns with broader wellness trends. Some of our student teams referenced biophilic packaging of products or design of spaces to provide sustainable and stress-less environments for diners or guests.

We had the chance to connect with Walk with Walsh founder Jennifer Walsh, whose mission is to have us change the way we look at nature. She strives to bring people outdoors into nature "to create more biophilic lifestyles." Green spaces and nature positively influence overall health and mental state. She leads wellness walks nationwide for individuals, hotels, brands, and corporations to "get everyone back outside." Nature ultimately became an important element of some of our marketing and activity recommendations.

We also learned about the global Wellness in Travel and Tourism (WITT) Certification, which provides a framework for hotels to align with global wellness standards. To earn certification, properties must meet criteria in five areas: healthy eating, holistic healing, nature integration, movement, and local impact. This certification ensures consistency and credibility while appealing to wellness-conscious travelers. It provides a uniform set of standards for hotels worldwide to be recognized as wellness-focused, ensuring offerings are both ambitious and attainable. These standards allow properties to provide a wide range of options that cater to all guests' varying needs and preferences.

We also learned that as the industry moves forward, the focus extends beyond traditional hotel guests to include outreach to the local community—social and lifestyle visitors, as well as business professionals.

Wellness is not just a trend but a transformative shift in how hospitality brands connect with locals and tourists, positioning themselves as a coveted third spot where individuals can seamlessly incorporate these establishments into their daily self-care routines.

Case Studies

By understanding two specific classroom efforts—The Mandarin Oriental, Boston, and Moxy Boston Downtown—we learn about innovative approaches to integrating wellness into brands. While The Mandarin Oriental Hotel, Boston embraces a holistic and luxurious approach rooted in its five-element philosophy, Moxy Boston injects its signature playful energy into offerings with bold and unconventional campaigns. Together, these examples highlight the on-brand marketing strategies that can redefine wellness in hospitality, catering to varied guest expectations and solidifying brand differentiation.

Mandarin Oriental Hotel, Boston: "Embrace the Elements for Your Personalized Path to Wellness"

The Mandarin Oriental Hotel, Boston (MOHB) has distinguished itself as a leader in wellness hospitality. In class, we studied how The Spa at MOHB leverages innovative marketing strategies to integrate health and balance seamlessly into the guest experience, thereby enhancing brand reputation and driving sustained growth.

MOHB has earned prestigious accolades such as *Forbes'* "Best Hotel for Wellness" and *Boston Magazine's* "Best Hotel, Wellness," positioning itself as a premier destination. Central to this recognition is The Spa, the longest-standing *Forbes*-rated #1 five-star spa in Massachusetts. Featuring eleven treatment rooms, including two couples' suites and a state-of-the-art fitness center, The Spa offers a comprehensive range of services designed to rejuvenate guests physically and mentally.

Despite its strong market position, there is an opportunity to extend the wellness experience beyond The Spa and further into the hotel stay. Currently, The Spa excels in attracting local clientele, with 85 percent of its guests coming from neighboring communities. To capitalize on this foundation, the marketing recommendations aim to engage hotel guests and owners of the Mandarin Oriental Hotel Residences, driving midweek traffic and reinforcing wellness as a core brand pillar. Key offerings include personalized massages, custom skincare treatments, retreats, Reiki energy healing, and a sleep concierge. Additionally, recent renovations to the fitness center and the introduction of exclusive memberships and personal training services further enhance the hotel's status as a full wellness destination.

The recommended marketing strategy was rooted in The Spa's current philosophy of the five elements: wood, fire, earth, metal, and water. This approach guides guests on a transformative and personalized journey, positioning The Spa at Mandarin Oriental, Boston as a leader in holistic luxury wellness and aligning with the broader Mandarin Oriental mission to "delight and inspire our fans at every opportunity." The recommendations utilized the elements already in place and simply elevated them.

Core Objectives (Of the Student-Driven Marketing Recommendations):

1. **Establish Wellness as a Brand Pillar:**
   Reinforce The Spa as synonymous with luxurious and holistic wellness experiences.

2. **Enhance Guest Engagement:**
   Offer tailored, element-inspired treatments and programs to foster deeper guest connections, enhancing satisfaction and loyalty.

3. **Increase Traffic to the Spa:**
   Attract both hotel guests and local clientele with unique and innovative wellness services.

Key Initiatives:

1. **Element-Inspired Offerings**
   - Signature Treatments: Develop spa treatments inspired by each of the five elements.

     - Wood: Detoxifying and energizing treatments to encourage growth and renewal.
     - Fire: Invigorating therapies that enhance vitality and passion.
     - Earth: Grounding rituals to promote stability and balance.
     - Metal: Purifying treatments that refine and restore.
     - Water: Hydrating and calming therapies for relaxation and reflection.

   - Guided Wellness Content: Introduce yoga, meditation, workout, and sleep videos through in-room entertainment systems, aligned with the five elements.

2. **Personalized Wellness Journeys**
   - The Spa Concierge: Launch a digital in-room app offering wellness assessments, real-time

booking, and exclusive personalized recommendations for treatments and wellness activities.

- Tailored Itineraries: Provide itineraries that integrate spa services, fitness classes, and dining experiences inspired by the five elements.

3. **Collaborative Experiences**

- Corporate Wellness Outreach: Implement wellness talks and "Lunch-and-Learn" sessions at local Boston offices, featuring healthy catered meals and presentations on The Spa's offerings, targeted at mindful managers to drive awareness and traffic.

4. **Content-Driven Marketing**

- Tagline Utilization: Use "Embrace the Elements for Your Personalized Path to Wellness" across all marketing campaigns.

- Multi-Channel Campaigns: Launch videos, blogs, and social media content educating audiences about the five elements and their integration into spa offerings.

- Authenticity Building: Showcase guest testimonials and behind-the-scenes content to build trust and authenticity.

5. **Seasonal Campaigns**

- Element-Specific Promotions: Align promotions with seasonal transitions, offering treatments and packages that resonate with the time of year. For example, spring promotions focus on wood-inspired offerings, emphasizing growth and renewal.

Implementation: The success of the marketing plan would be measured through various metrics, including:

- Midweek Spa Bookings: Tracking the increase in spa reservations during typically slower periods
- Digital Engagement: Monitoring interactions with digital content, including app usage and social media engagement
- Guest Satisfaction: Assessing overall guest satisfaction through surveys and feedback mechanisms
- Spa Revenue Growth: Evaluating year-over-year increases in spa-related revenue

The MOHB's strategic focus on integrating wellness into every aspect of the guest experience exemplifies the future of hospitality, where innovation, sustainability, and wellness converge to meet evolving guest expectations. By embracing the five elements and leveraging personalized, data-driven marketing strategies, the students delivered an approach for The Spa to enhance guest satisfaction while building intangible ROI through long-term loyalty and brand prestige.

Wellness Integration and Marketing Strategy for Moxy, Boston: "Turning Wellness on its A**"

Moxy Boston Downtown, in the heart of the city's Theater District, combines sleek design, a playful atmosphere, and ample opportunities for social connections. With 340 cleverly designed guest rooms and an industrial-chic second-floor social hub featuring a check-in bar, inviting lounges, and game zones, Moxy offers a unique experience for travelers seeking nightlife, local culture, and modern comfort.

Core Objectives: How do we incorporate wellness as a pillar of Moxy Boston Downtown's bold identity by integrating it into the guest experience? The goal is to create an energizing and memorable stay that differentiates Moxy from the competitive boutique hotel market by catering to the growing demand for wellness-focused amenities. The hotel already has a strong brand image for "fun" and "the unexpected." So, how can we integrate wellness and remain brand aligned?

Strategy: Moxy "Turning Wellness on Its A**"

This innovative campaign infuses Moxy's signature bold and playful energy into wellness experiences, blending self-care with socialization. The recommended strategy included:

- Rooftop Fitness Memberships: Offering unlimited access to fitness classes with stunning rooftop views
- In-Room Wellness Kits: Personalized kits addressing post-nightlife recovery
- Energizing Menu Options: Nutrient-rich foods to support guests' well-being
- Community Engagement: Partnerships showcasing Boston's local wellness scene

Implementation: There were three suggested initiatives to develop this initiative:

1. **"Join the MA**es" Membership**
   - Target Audience: Moxy's Social Seekers and Remote Workers.
   - Features: Unlimited access to rooftop fitness classes, including yoga, meditation, and silent disco cycling. Personalized membership cards that track participation and preferences. Access to select hotel amenities to enhance the overall experience.
   - Promotion: Digital platforms and influencers. Social media campaigns using hashtags like #JoinThe(M)asses and #MoveYourAss.

Instagram posts highlight rooftop views and vibrant class energy.

2. **"Revive Your A** Kit"**

- Purpose: Increase guest participation in evening events by offering wellness incentives.
- Contents: Liquid IV for hydration. Emergen-C for reducing hangover severity. Ginger tea for soothing digestive issues. Juice Press cookies for an energy boost. Sleep eye masks for restorative sleep. Condoms to promote safe nightlife experiences.
- Promotion: In-room TV messaging with QR codes for event calendars. Encourage guests to ask for yoga mats available at the front desk.

3. **In-Room and Lobby Visibility**

- In-Room Messaging: Promote wellness programs and encourage guests to utilize yoga mats.
- Visible Yoga Mat Display: Strategically placed behind the front desk to spark guest interest.
- Staff Training: Equip front desk staff to inform and engage guests about wellness offerings.

Execution Strategy:

- In-Room Messaging: TV displays would feature engaging content about wellness programs and direct guests to inquire about yoga mats.

- Visible Display of Yoga Mats: Positioned behind the front desk to act as a visual cue for guests.

- Staff Training: Ensure staff are knowledgeable and proactive in promoting wellness activities and memberships.

- Social Media Campaigns: Utilize visually appealing posts and strategic hashtags to enhance visibility and engagement.

Results and Expected Outcomes include:

- Increased Guest Engagement: Enhanced wellness class and evening event participation through targeted marketing and accessible amenities.

- Brand Differentiation: Moxy Boston Downtown stands out in the boutique hotel market by offering a unique blend of wellness and social experiences.

- Data-Driven Personalization: Membership cards track guest preferences, allowing for tailored offerings and improved loyalty.

- Community Connection: Strengthened ties with the local Boston wellness scene, attracting health-conscious travelers and locals alike.

By aligning wellness initiatives with their respective brand ethos, both properties can further elevate the guest experience and enhance their market positioning and loyalty. These examples illustrate the importance of creative, guest-centric strategies in meeting the growing demand for wellness offerings to drive brand differentiation with long-term success.

Incorporating Innovation and Impact into Marketing

Below are a few actionable strategies to help us infuse social impact into our business approaches:

1. **Embed the Value in Brand Messaging and Product Development:**
   Marketers should collaborate with product teams to ensure sustainability/wellness/community engagement isn't just a marketing message, but a core belief reflected in the product or service itself. In campaigns, highlight tangible actions, such as using eco-friendly materials or reducing carbon footprints. Transparency is key. Share measurable goals and progress to build credibility with consumers.

2. **Partner with Local Communities for Mutual Growth:**
   Build partnerships with local organizations, non-profits, or community leaders to create initiatives that benefit both the community and the brand. Marketing these partnerships

authentically, through storytelling and highlighting real community impact, demonstrates a genuine commitment to CSR.

3. **Incorporate Innovation in Customer Engagement:**

   Leverage technology to engage customers around sustainability and social responsibility. For example, use augmented reality (AR) or interactive digital experiences to educate audiences on your brand's sustainability practices. This creates a memorable and engaging way to communicate your CSR efforts.

4. **Encourage Employee Involvement and Advocacy:**

   Foster a culture where employees actively participate in sustainability or community initiatives. Whether through volunteering, sustainability task forces, or internal challenges, involving employees helps integrate CSR into the company's DNA. Encourage employees to share their experiences on social media to amplify these messages authentically.

5. **Create Campaigns that Inspire Consumer Action:**

   Develop campaigns that invite participation in sustainability efforts, such as recycling programs, donation drives, or cause-related challenges. Offering incentives or matching contributions can further boost engagement and strengthen brand loyalty.

Marketing Mindset for the Future

Shifting gears slightly, let's address other potential evolutions for the future of marketing and communications. When we chatted for our school's *Boston Hospitality Review*, Julie Freeman and her MMGY team articulated several theories and insights about the future of marketing approaches. I include them here because I wholeheartedly agree. What do you think?

1. **Traditional PR Will Not Exist as We've Known It.**

   Gone are the days of "tried and true PR tactics." Clients will rely on our creative ideas, partnerships, and strategic counsel to connect them to consumers, tapping into deep media relationships worldwide to reimagine how stories are told. Trends will come and go more quickly than ever before. Journalists will constantly write for new outlets or cover new beats. Media won't necessarily live domestically and might write for outlets in several other countries. Editorial calendars built out a year in advance will be useless. It will be about tapping into timely and opportunistic moments to capture attention. PR teams will need to be nimbler and more aware of the trends and the changing media landscape than ever before to keep up with moving the needle for clients, consumers, and media. Successful PR teams will be those that create innovative, interactive, and bespoke experiences to share their clients' narratives with media, influencers, and consumers.

2. **Multi-Channel, One Voice.**

   It will become more important than ever that our work is part of an entire marketing eco-sphere. Our efforts will mirror marketing's efforts, but marketing will also need to amplify our work. There is already a great blend between PR and media and content, and those lines will continue to blur. Our work and mission will continue to be the same; we will provide truthful, authentic information that inspires. PR must be 100 percent fully integrated with broadcast, social, experiential, partnerships, and marketing platforms, as the media landscape will be fully digital. Agencies, already ingrained with full-service capabilities and big-picture thinking, will lend seamlessly to a steady transition.

3. **Digital Storytelling is Key, and It is Global.**

   Digital stories and online video coverage will be the future of all client coverage. PR will transition to a full-service paid and earned outlook.[8] More owned, more virtual, more brands using social media for PR, and more podcasting are the future of public relations and marketing communications. Looking at the historic trend, we will see an ongoing shift from long-form journalism to roundups and listicles. We have already begun incorporating digital video assets with pitches for posting on the outlets' websites and social pages to drive views and engagement. Outlets are creating videos from still images for stories we secure. Because media outlets will be all digital, content becomes global. To maintain their relevance, savvy media organizations have introduced new content platforms and revenue streams to survive and attempt to thrive in this new era of media.

4. **Social Media and Journalism Will Continue to Blend.**

   With the shrinking newsroom came a further blending of journalism and social media. For example, with fewer travel editors and less budget to cover freelancers, hosting of "social editors" from top publications on press trips has been on the rise. These social editors wear multiple hats, yielding both editorial and social media coverage. In addition, many freelance travel journalists have launched Substacks or newsletters to have ownership over their content.

5. **Influencers will Continue to Influence.**

   More time and resources will be spent on influencer relations. Public relations must be adaptable and open to exploring new media, such as earned influencers. We will continue to see a rise in paid influencers, but clients will expect us to work seamlessly with unpaid influencers as part of our scope and budget.

6. **Pay-for-Play, Advertorials,[9] and Affiliate Marketing Will Play a Larger Role.**

   We will be navigating fewer "free" sources of news media, making it difficult to place wide-ranging messages and increasing the disparity between those who have access to resources and those who don't. Media outlets will want more dollars and incentives to write about clients in the years ahead.

A Vision Forward

The future of marketing is poised to become more personalized, data-driven, and immersive. Advanced analytics and artificial intelligence will enable market-ers to understand and anticipate consumer behaviors with better precision, allowing for highly targeted and relevant campaigns. The rise of virtual and augmented reality will create immersive brand experiences that engage customers in novel ways, fostering deeper con-nections and loyalty. Integrating sustainable and ethical practices into marketing strategies will resonate with a more socially conscious audience, enhancing brand repu-tation and trust.

I urge hospitality and all service businesses to connect with your constituents through messages of caring about their well-being and sustainability for a more purposeful connection. This results in a (hopefully, authentic and) profound marketing effort that cuts through the clutter of existing noise.

The Vision Comes with Marketing Challenges

While emerging tools and strategies offer exciting opportunities, they also present obstacles that must be thoughtfully navigated to ensure long-term success and trust. Consider the following issues:

As marketing becomes increasingly personalized and data-driven, privacy regulations like GDPR (General Data Protection Regulation) and CCPA (California Consumer Privacy Act) present challenges in collecting, storing, and using consumer data. Consumers are also more aware of how their data is used, increasing the need for *transparency* and ethical handling of information.

It's important to remember the necessity of communicating transparently about data usage, showing customers how their data enhances their experience while safeguarding their privacy.

With the rise of advanced technology such as AI-driven content and immersive experiences, marketers may struggle to balance innovation with the authenticity that consumers demand. When we rely too heavily on technology, the message can lose that personal, genuine touch.

As marketers, we must remember that storytelling remains at the core of marketing efforts, using technology to enhance, not replace, human connection. Employees and customers will be more empowered to share authentic stories through user-generated content (UGC) and brand advocacy programs. And naturally, we must regularly evaluate campaigns to ensure they reflect the brand's purpose, values, and voice.

The pace of innovation in marketing technology (MarTech), including virtual reality (VR), augmented reality (AR), and artificial intelligence (AI), can overwhelm marketers, making it difficult to choose the right tools and platforms. We will need to focus on strategic adoption of technology and only invest in tools that align with our business goals and/or enhance our customer experience. So, it is important to provide ongoing training and upskilling for marketing teams to stay current with emerging technologies.

With shorter attention spans and a deluge of competing content (noise), it's harder than ever to capture and retain customer attention, let alone guide them through the stages of awareness, interest, and loyalty. We, as marketers and communicators, must create "digestible," bite-sized, highly engaging content tailored to each stage of the customer decision-making journey—awareness, interest, desire, action, retention—and use dynamic formats, such as short videos, interactive posts, and personalized emails.

And as consumers become more socially conscious, we must integrate sustainability and ethical practices into strategies without appearing opportunistic. Creating internal, or external, cross-functional teams can ensure genuine CSR efforts are built into the core of the business, not just its marketing. Highlighting measurable impacts with data and case studies can show real progress on sustainability and ethical initiatives, proving an authentic offering to customers or guests.

We must implement a truth-first policy in all marketing communications, ensuring claims are fact-checked and substantiated before going live. Using agile marketing practices to maintain speed while preserving accuracy, with built-in review processes that prioritize quality over quantity, will also help encourage internal alignment by involving cross-functional teams (think about the product development and legal departments) early in the marketing process to ensure consistent, truthful messaging.

The future of marketing presents exciting opportunities, but it also requires us to navigate complex challenges with thoughtfulness, agility, and integrity. Marketers can successfully guide brands through this ever-evolving world by embracing innovation and staying true to our core values, such as trust and authenticity, while surfacing wellness, sustainability and community engagement for more meaningful connection.

Marketing Mantras

While I have consistently advocated for incorporating elements of corporate social responsibility into marketing plans, I now teach that it is not merely an option but a necessity. Today, all marketing initiatives must inherently and authentically contribute to the wellness of guests or individuals or promote the well-being of communities, environments, or the planet. Integrating wellness and sustainability is no longer an afterthought; it is fundamental to the essence of hospitality marketing strategies.

1. **Innovate to Meet Customers' Needs:**

    As stated several times throughout these pages, and as Marc Mazodier so directly shared with me for the *Boston Hospitality Review*, "In my opinion, strong marketing is when innovation meets consumers' needs."

2. **Shift Your Perspective on Innovation:**

    Innovation in hospitality goes beyond adopting the latest technologies; it encompasses the creation of unique offerings and inventive marketing strategies that strengthen relationships with both employees and guests, enhancing their well-being or that of the community around them.

3. **Integrate Genuine Sustainable Practices:**

    Sustainability should be viewed as a fundamental obligation rather than a mere trend. Hospitality businesses must embed environmentally responsible practices into their operations, from energy-efficient systems to waste reduction initiatives. Authentic sustainability efforts minimize environmental impact and resonate with increasingly eco-conscious consumers. Actively communicate these initiatives through transparent and meaningful marketing to establish trust and loyalty.

4. **Adopt a CSR mindset:**

   By prioritizing CSR, hospitality businesses can enhance their brand reputation, attract socially conscious consumers, and create genuine connections. Marketing efforts should highlight how the business contributes to the well-being of people, places, and the planet, reiterating the brand's dedication to making a positive difference.

5. **Prioritize Privacy and Build Trust:**

   We must adopt a privacy-first approach, ensuring transparency in how we collect, store, and use data. We must actively communicate the value of data collection to our customers and safeguard their privacy to strengthen trust.

6. **Leverage Technology to Enhance Human Connection:**

   Let's use advanced tools like AI and immersive technologies to amplify, not replace, human connection. When we combine innovation with authentic storytelling, we create memorable marketing experiences.

> Wellness is that of an individual's mind,
> body, spirit, and soul.
> Sustainability is the wellness of people,
> place, and the planet.

As we conclude our look at some of these dynamic issues, it is equally important to ground our strategies in a few of my favorite perspectives about hospitality. In the final chapter, we take a glance at some of the core values and diverse approaches that define true hospitality, ensuring that the next generation of marketers and professionals remains dedicated to creating memorable and heartfelt experiences for every guest.

Mindset in Motion

The future of hospitality marketing hinges on innovation, sustainability (including wellness and community engagement), and evolving consumer expectations. How can brands stay ahead while remaining authentic? Consider the impact of AI, personalization, and experiential marketing. What strategies resonate most for your business, employees, and customers? How do sustainability and wellness initiatives shape brand perception and long-term success? Outline a forward-thinking approach that balances innovation with your brand's core values. How will it make people feel (that's the hospitality element)? What's your vision for the future, and how will you navigate its challenges and opportunities?

The Marketing Mindset Scorecard
Contemporary and Future-Focused Marketing

Chapter 9

Milestone: From Following Trends to Innovating and Leading

Concept	1 (Needs Work)	3 (Getting There)	5 (Fully Integrated)
Embracing Innovation	I stick to traditional methods	I try new approaches but hesitate to take risks	I test, adapt, and innovate in marketing strategies
Sustainability and CSR Integration	I see sustainability as a PR move	I understand its business value, but don't prioritize it	I integrate sustainability authentically into marketing strategies

Reflection Questions:

- Are you proactively exploring and testing new marketing tools and innovations?
- How are you integrating sustainability and corporate responsibility into marketing?

10

Remember the Hospitality

Throughout my career, I've had the privilege of learning from and being inspired by remarkable "philosophers" of hospitality whose messages continue to resonate with me. I strive to impart these meaningful mantras to my students, believing in their power and witnessing their impact firsthand. The concepts shared here show how we can create memorable and remarkable experiences that lift the human connection in hospitality and elevate our marketing to communicate accordingly.

"Surprise and Delight:" Brand Examples

Creating moments of joy is essential for fostering memorable customer experiences. These moments go beyond meeting expectations; they exceed them, leaving a lasting impression that cultivates loyalty and positive word-of-mouth. This means personalized, unexpected gestures that build strong ties and feelings result in memorable, remarkable experiences with surprise and delight moments.

ITT Sheraton: I first heard the term "surprise and delight" when I worked on-property for Sheraton Hotels in New York. It was part of our extensive and outstanding ongoing training. How can we think ahead to connect with a guest, customer, or patron and make them feel special by interacting with our business, product, or service? It's not easy, but when it goes well, it goes *really* well. How does a concierge suddenly access theater tickets to allow a guest a special mother-daughter weekend? How does a restaurant server overhear a conversation and immediately return with a large, hot, steamy, and salty New York pretzel to present to the table and conclude their meal? How does a healthcare worker find just the right thing to say to a patient or a senior living resident to start that person's morning with a smile and set the tone for a wonderful day? How can a salesperson in a department store or boutique know just what clothes to show a customer, or even know when to stop engaging to give that person the time they need, and then suddenly appear with exactly what they were looking for?

Disney: A simple, yet excellent, example of "surprise and delight" comes from Disney. At their theme parks, employees, known as "cast members," are trained to look for opportunities to create *magical moments* for guests.

For instance, if a child is celebrating a birthday, a cast member may present them with a complimentary birthday pin and lead a chorus of "Happy Birthday." This simple gesture makes the child's day and creates a ripple effect, as parents and other guests witness the attention to detail and care. The effectiveness of this action lies in its ability to personalize the experience, making the child feel special and valued in a crowded amusement park.

From a customer experience perspective, this approach demonstrates that the little things matter. Disney fosters connections that drive repeat visits by anticipating guests' needs and celebrating milestones. This principle can be applied across various industries. For instance, a boutique hotel might leave a handwritten note and a small gift in the room for a couple celebrating their anniversary. Such gestures create a sense of belonging and appreciation, enhancing the overall experience.

Chewy: Chewy has built its reputation on exceptional customer service, often going above and beyond to create memorable experiences for pet owners. For instance, when a customer orders a pet food product and mentions a pet's name in the order notes, Chewy's customer service team may take the extra step to send a customized note or a special treat for the pet along with their order. This small gesture shows that Chewy cares about the customer and reinforces the bond between the owner and their beloved pet. And nothing can come between a pet parent and their dog or cat.

This approach to customer service demonstrates a key marketing lesson: the power of connecting individually. By creating a unique experience for each customer, Chewy transforms a simple transaction into a heartfelt engagement, boosting brand loyalty and encouraging repeat purchases.

From a broader marketing perspective, the effectiveness of Chewy's actions lies in their ability to connect with their customers in a heartfelt manner. When customers feel valued and understood, they are more likely to share their positive experiences with others, both on and offline. This word-of-mouth marketing is incredibly powerful, as personal recommendations often influence potential customers more than traditional advertising.

We recently lost our family dog of thirteen years, our beautiful little girl, Charli. When we called Chewy to tell them we no longer needed the automatic food delivery, they immediately credited the last month's order even though we received it. They told us not to send it back to them but to donate it to a vet or animal hospital instead, which we did. They were so gracious and compassionate in expressing their condolences; it was meaningful and helpful during our grief. I'd certainly recommend Chewy to our family and friends for their dogs. A few days later, a beautiful flower bouquet arrived at our home with a personalized note of condolence. Chewy cares about my dog-loving family.

Marketers and hospitality professionals, please prioritize individual connection in customer interactions. Consider how you can enrich your customers with unexpected gestures that show you truly understand their needs and preferences. Whether it's through meaningful notes, unexpected value-added offers, or small gifts, these actions can elevate the customer experience and foster lasting loyalty.

"The Amtrak Man:" One of my more recent and memorable moments comes from Jermaine, an Amtrak manager at New York's Moynihan Station. I have seen him in action for nearly a decade, engaging with travelers waiting for their trains. I've heard his loud, cheerful voice guiding passengers, ensuring they board their trains with a smile.

On Labor Day in 2024, the station was bustling with commuters eager to return to their routines. As I waited in the lobby level public area, Jermaine excitedly engaged a group of passengers heading to Boston, enthusiastically recommending a restaurant called Eastern Standard and shouting the name of its owner, Garrett Harker. *How does he know Eastern Standard or Garrett,* I wondered? Intrigued, I waited to speak with him after the crowd dispersed, asking how he knew about the restaurant and its famed operator.

With a grin, Jermaine looked at me and asked, "You know Garrett?" When I confirmed I did, he suggested we take a selfie to send to him. I was shocked; he had

Garrett's cell number? Jermaine walked me to the train platform and proceeded to bring me onto the train and help me settle into my seat, wishing me a great day and encouraging me to do the same for others. It was VIP treatment.

About a week later, I dined at Eastern Standard with two of my former students, and when Garrett approached, I excitedly shared the selfie and asked, "How do you know the Amtrak Man?" Garrett smiled and chuckled aloud. I learned that Jermaine genuinely uplifted Garrett during a tough day at the train station in New York, which led to a lasting friendship and even a couple of motivational speaking opportunities for Jermaine. Garrett knew Jermaine was special within minutes of meeting him, and their connection transformed both their lives.

Jermaine's mission is to spread positivity and encourage others to do good. He continues to motivate passengers by treating everyone as a VIP, embodying the spirit of hospitality through his infectious energy and kindness. I've seen it blessed onto others and experienced it firsthand.

This story illustrates the essence of bringing unanticipated joy into customer experiences. Jermaine's sincere interactions foster relationship building, showing that creating memorable moments can even lead to lasting friendship. His spirit of "surprise and delight" and his ability to reassure and inspire passengers brighten our day and create a ripple effect of positivity. Businesses should empower their employees to engage authentically with customers, as these heartfelt interactions lead to lasting impressions and cultivate a loyal community.

Danny Meyer's Enlightened Hospitality

I'm a fan. I've been a fan of this man's restaurants for as long as I can remember, and I've been a fan of how he practices and delivers hospitality. Danny Meyer is a visionary restaurateur and the acclaimed founder of Union Square Hospitality Group (USHG), one of New York City's most esteemed and influential companies. Having built a legacy of excellence, Danny has transformed the dining landscape through his innovative approach to restaurant management and exceptional service standards. Under his leadership and the inspiration of his partner and longtime friend, the incomparable human saint, Richard Coraine (RC), USHG has launched a portfolio of celebrated establishments, including the iconic Union Square Café, Gramercy Tavern, and one of my faves, Ci Siamo. And then, of course, there's Shake Shack. As Shake Shack's founder and visionary leader, Danny leveraged his extensive experience to transform a simple hot dog cart into a global fast-casual phenomenon. His commitment to excellence and his ability to create memorable dining experiences have earned him numerous accolades, solidifying his reputation as a pioneer in the culinary and hospitality industries.

Danny Meyer's groundbreaking philosophy of *Enlightened Hospitality* is at the heart of his success. This

approach redefines traditional hospitality by emphasizing the well-being of employees and guests. Unlike
conventional models that prioritize profit margins and
operational efficiency, Enlightened Hospitality fosters
a culture of respect, empathy, and genuine care within
the workplace. Danny, in his book, *Setting the Table* (a
must-read for all in our industry or any service industry,
for that matter), believes that by valuing and nurturing
his team members, they, in turn, deliver exceptional service to guests, creating a virtuous cycle of positivity and
excellence. So, the guest doesn't necessarily come first.
The employee does.

Among the core principles of Enlightened Hospitality
are lessons that teach us to:

- **Serve the employees first:**
  Danny's philosophy begins with the belief that
  happy, well-treated employees are the foundation
  of outstanding customer service. Companies can
  ensure that their team feels valued and motivated
  by investing in staff through comprehensive
  training, competitive wages, and a supportive
  work environment.
- **Create memorable guest experiences:**
  Enlightened Hospitality strives to exceed customer expectations—not just meet them—by
  creating memorable experiences. We must
  encourage our teams to anticipate guests' needs,

pay attention to the smallest details, and engage in meaningful interactions.

- **Cultivate a culture of continuous improvement:**

  Advocate for a dynamic and adaptive workplace where feedback is actively sought and embraced. A company continuously evolves through open communication and encourages innovative ideas to meet changing customer preferences and industry trends.

- **Emphasize community and connection:**

  Enlightened Hospitality also involves building strong connections within the community and fostering a sense of belonging among guests. Companies that believe in the power of relationships and strive to create spaces where people can come together enhance their reputation and strengthen their presence.

I have read *Setting the Table* three times (so far). Each time, I've underlined different quotes or scenarios that resonated with me at that moment. I've flipped down the corners of different pages each time I've read the book. I have been fortunate to meet Danny on several occasions. I've also participated in his Hospitality Quotient training, where I received another copy of his book—this time, signed and, of course, personalized. I will treasure that book always.

"If you ask me what phrase I remember most from class, one I keep repeating to everyone who asks me the question, 'What is hospitality?' I say, 'It is all about the people.'

"Also, from my class project, I learned to appeal to emotions, especially if I want to connect with that person. Yes, content, research, and creativity are indeed important, but what people truly remember from the time they spend with you is *how you made them feel.* I've been extremely passionate about this, and it was deeply reinforced during my time working at Union Square Hospitality Group (USHG)."

—Richard Peet Hannah,
BU School of Hospitality, Class of 2022

Will Guidara's Unreasonable Hospitality

Now for the book that is truly the must-read—what I call "the sequel" to Danny Meyer's *Setting the Table: Unreasonable Hospitality.* In this book, Will Guidara pushes the importance of hospitality as a key element of his restaurants' culture even further by encouraging his team to think creatively and proactively about how to *exhilarate* guests. He pushes us to focus on the unexpected moments that transform a standard dining experience into a memorable event.

The incomparable Brian Lesser in Boston, the man behind many of the city's most prominent restaurants, said to me one evening, "*You* need to read this book." If Brian suggests I read a book, I'll order it on Amazon that night. And I did, and I read the book in one glorious weekend. It's incredible.

Will Guidara is best known for his pivotal role in transforming Eleven Madison Park in New York City into one of the world's most celebrated dining establishments and, ultimately, the Number One Restaurant in the World. A protégé of Danny Meyer, Guidara's innovative approach to hospitality, which he titled "unreasonable," emphasizes exceptional customer experiences.

Will was twenty-six when he took the helm of Eleven Madison Park, then a struggling two-star brasserie. Eleven years later, the restaurant was named the best in the world. As his book explains, he accomplished this through "radical reinvention, a true partnership between the kitchen and the dining room, and memorable, over-the-top hospitality."

For example, Will and his team stunned a family who had never seen snow with a magical sledding trip to Central Park after their dinner; they filled a private dining room with sand, complete with mai-tais and beach chairs, to console a couple with a cancelled vacation. And his hospitality extended beyond those dining at the restaurant to his team, who learned to deliver praise and criticism with intention.

As shared in this book, every business can choose to be a hospitality business, and everyone should learn how to "transform ordinary transactions into extraordinary experiences."

"Unreasonable hospitality" is the power of giving people more than they expect by finding magic in what you do. It's about going above and beyond traditional expectations to create memorable experiences by infusing generosity, creativity, and genuine care into every interaction and transaction. Attention to detail is key because minor actions can have a lasting impact. And valuing and investing in employees builds a healthy culture for any business. Other themes I gained from the book involve resilience, adaptability, and maintaining a positive outlook in the face of adversity.

Guidara's storytelling brilliance in the book makes this an easy read, and if anyone watches *The Bear*, you'll recognize one of Will's stories in Season 2, Episode 7, called "Forks." In this episode, Cousin Richie stages at a fictional three-Michelin-starred restaurant called Ever, where he learns from the book *Unreasonable Hospitality*. In "Forks," Richie's first task is to polish forks, but he eventually learns to connect with his co-workers and the rhythms of the restaurant. He returns to The Bear (the sandwich shop turned fine dining restaurant) with a new attitude about professionalism, even wearing a suit to work. The episode also features a scene of a team member running out to a Chicago hot dog cart to bring back a perfectly garnished hot dog to a table of guests (because he overheard the guests saying they didn't get to eat a Chicago hot dog during their trip). This was right out of the book! Brilliant. Guidara served as co-producer for the series that season, co-writing storylines, and even appearing in the final episode, bringing authentic portrayals of the culinary world.

Will Guidara believes that every interaction offers an opportunity to exceed expectations, and he empowers his staff to embrace this philosophy. For hospitality professionals looking to implement these principles, prioritize customization and creativity in every guest interaction. The marketing will take it from there. And for professionals in other industries where we interact with people, which is every industry, we should do the same.

Experience Innovation: Redefining 21st Century Hospitality

During the pandemic, the faculty at BU's School of Hospitality met several times to ensure our curriculum kept ahead of the curve and adapted to meet the changing needs of guests in a new era. We brought hospitality to new heights, knowing we had embarked on a more experience-driven society. *Experience Innovation* represents an elevated hospitality application, where cutting-edge solutions and creative approaches streamline operations and elevate the overall guest journey, ensuring sustained growth and exceptional satisfaction in an increasingly competitive market. We position

Experience Innovation as a business differentiator for forward-thinking businesses.

With Experience Innovation, students learn to craft seamless digital and physical interactions that transform customer loyalty, optimize service touch points, and foster adaptability. Students navigate evolving consumer expectations and learn how disruptive innovation impacts service delivery, resulting in a sense of adaptability and resilience in creating these outstanding experiences. We apply design thinking principles to craft user-centered service solutions using techniques like journey mapping and service blueprinting. Through empathy-driven problem-solving, case studies, and real-world applications, we analyze successful service innovations across industries, gaining insights into personalizing experiences for customers and employees alike. This philosophy sets us apart from other hospitality educational programs as well.

Just Be Kind

Mentioned earlier, David Gibbons was the executive director of the Massachusetts Convention Center Authority (MCCA). A lifelong hospitality and hotel executive, David is a wonderful person who participated in my classes more than once because he was eager to gain insights from fresh minds.

One semester, he challenged our students to research why hotels were less cooperative in booking rooms for incoming large association business and conventions (years in advance) when a guaranteed block of rooms was sold and guaranteed for future dates. The students conducted interviews as part of their due diligence to understand the RFP (request for proposal) process for convention groups. They reached out to the MCCA and then connected with hotel representatives to determine whether the issue was a communication gap or a reluctance from hotel owners to book lower-rated rooms so far in advance.

The students discovered a genuine desire to help from hotel salespeople, but they didn't feel the love back from the MCCA. The MCCA needed to simply say "thank you" and build relationships with these sales managers. This approach would prevent the work from feeling transactional and unappreciated, fostering a true win-win situation in the booking business.

"Thank you." This is something we should never take for granted or assume. The students recommended a series of annual thank-you events for the various tourism stakeholders who worked with the MCCA to ensure success. David was kind enough to invite me to the first of these events a semester after our student team proposed the idea and then graduated. I videotaped the event and emailed it to our (then) alumni to demonstrate that our industry treasures their insights and listens to them. The MCCA implemented many of the students' suggestions.

Boy, the power of a simple "thank you."

Each semester, on the last day of classes, I ask students to share some of their favorite takeaways from our course-work. One year, student Clare Jun raised her hand and asked me, "What advice would you have for us as we graduate and enter the working world?" I knew I had shared many lessons in class, so I didn't want to respond with another lecture. Instead, I simply said, "Be kind."

The Ultimate Marketing Mantra

As we explored the ways to shape a marketing mind-set within the hospitality industry, I shared some of the essential and practical principles I teach in my courses. They can be applied to a wide range of service- and people-focused businesses. From retail, where customer relationships are paramount, to country clubs catering to members, senior living communities taking care of residents, and even banking and insurance firms creating relationships with customers, the lessons drawn from hospitality offer valuable insights for any business involving interactions and exchanges with people.

Cultivating a marketing mindset has proven essential for navigating challenges and seizing opportunities across various contexts. Throughout this book, we have journeyed through various approaches to contemporary issues, such as sustainability, wellness, innovation and community connection. Each chapter emphasizes the significance of critical thinking, strategic targeting of messaging, understanding the customers' desires and wants, relationship-building, and effective communication while crafting memorable experiences and marketing them effectively, while inadvertently marketing ourselves along the way.

So, what is a marketing mindset? It is a holistic approach that merges strategic thinking with practical execution. This mindset involves thinking like a marketer and acting like an owner, understanding the nuances of brand identity and experience, leveraging the power of relationships over mere transactions, and staying adaptable to contemporary issues. It emphasizes a deep understanding of the *why* behind our actions, the importance of customized experiences, and the continuous evolution of marketing practices in a dynamic environment. Marketing means providing a customer solution.

And the lessons from hospitality? Our marketing mindset fosters a strategic, yet empathetic approach focused on creating extraordinary guest experiences. It requires a keen understanding of brand identity and a commitment to personalization and building lasting relationships. Businesses can thrive by prioritizing exceptional service and remaining attuned to the latest industry innovations and guest expectations.

As we adopt a marketing mindset from hospitality, we empower ourselves to create value for our organizations and our communities. Adopting this mindset is key to succeeding in today's fast-paced, constantly evolving world. By applying the insights and recommendations shared throughout this book, we can cultivate a marketing mindset that resonates across industries, enhancing our marketing strategies and the overall experiences we provide to those we serve.

Mindset in Motion

At its core, great marketing is great hospitality; it's about making people feel seen, valued, and cared for. Think about the most memorable brand experience you've had. What made it stand out? Reflect on examples like Disney's attention to detail, Chewy's personal touch, or Will Guidara's philosophy of Unreasonable Hospitality. How can you bring this mindset into your work? Whether through small gestures or big innovations, how will you create moments of surprise and delight that leave a lasting impact? In the end, the ultimate marketing mantra is simple: Just be kind. How will you embody this in your approach?

The Marketing Mindset Scorecard

Remembering the Hospitality

Chapter 10

Milestone: From Transactional Marketing to Creating Meaningful Connections

Concept	1 (Needs Work)	3 (Getting There)	5 (Fully Integrated)
Surprise and Delight	I focus on selling, not delighting customers	I see the value in personalization, but struggle with execution	I consistently create experiences that make customers feel valued
Hospitality as a Business Mindset	I don't consider hospitality in marketing	I acknowledge its value, but don't always apply it	I actively use hospitality principles in all customer interactions

Reflection Questions:

- Do you create marketing strategies that genuinely make customers feel special?
- Have you embraced hospitality as an essential business mindset, not just for hospitality brands?

11

Reviewing the Marketing Mindset Scorecard

Throughout *Developing Your Marketing Mindset: Real-World Lessons from Hospitality*, we've tracked progress using a Marketing Mindset Scorecard. As we conclude, it's time to reflect on how our understanding has evolved.

As we've self-assessed across key concepts, we've gained insight into marketing as a strategic discipline and the importance of a hospitality-driven approach. This final review allows us to see where we've grown, identify areas for further development, and solidify our marketing mindset for future success.

Looking Back at Our Progress:

- How have our ratings shifted from the start to now?
- Which areas feel strongest, and where do we still have room to grow?
- How will we apply this mindset in our daily work moving forward?

Let's take a final look at the scorecard and the key take-aways from each section.

1. Cultivating the Marketing Mindset: Critical and Strategic Thinking

Chapters 1–6

Milestone: From Awareness to Strategic Thinking

Concept	1 (Needs Work)	3 (Getting There)	5 (Fully Integrated)
Thinking Like a Marketer, Acting Like an Owner	I focus on tactics, not strategy	I consider ROI, but struggle to connect tactics to strategy	I align marketing with business objectives and ROI

Understanding Your Why	I market without a clear purpose	I see the importance of why, but struggle to define it	I start every strategy with a clear purpose
Brand and Experience Connection	I view branding as a logo or slogan	I recognize the role of customer experience in branding	I build brands with experiences that reinforce authenticity
Strategic Goal Setting	I set vague goals without measurement	I track goals but struggle with meaningful KPIs	I define clear, measurable goals and refine them based on data

Reflection Questions:

- Have you shifted from executing tactics to thinking about long-term strategy?
- Can you articulate the why behind a brand's marketing strategy?
- Are you considering customer experience as a core part of your brand positioning?

2. Marketing Yourself

Chapters 7 and 8

Milestone: From Passive Presence to Personal Brand Advocate

Concept	1 (Needs Work)	3 (Getting There)	5 (Fully Integrated)
Personal Branding	I don't actively manage my professional image	I have an online presence, but I don't optimize it or keep it fresh	I consciously build and refine my professional brand
Staying Current and Connected	I rarely engage with market-ing trends or network	I follow trends but don't engage in conversations	I read, network, and contribute thought leadership

Reflection Questions:

- Are you consciously shaping your professional brand or leaving it to chance?
- How often do you invest in learning new mar-keting trends and skills?

3. Contemporary and Future-Focused Marketing

Chapter 9

Milestone: From Following Trends to Innovating and Leading

Concept	1 (Needs Work)	3 (Getting There)	5 (Fully Integrated)
Embracing Innovation	I stick to traditional methods	I try new approaches but hesitate to take risks	I test, adapt, and innovate in marketing strategies
Sustainability and CSR Integration	I see sustainability as a PR move	I understand its business value, but don't prioritize it	I integrate sustainability authentically into marketing strategies

Reflection Questions:

- Are you proactively exploring and testing new marketing tools and innovations?
- How are you integrating sustainability and corporate responsibility into marketing?

4. Remembering the Hospitality

Chapter 10

Milestone: From Transactional Marketing to Creating
Meaningful Connections

Concept	1 (Needs Work)	3 (Getting There)	5 (Fully Integrated)
Surprise and Delight	I focus on selling, not delighting customers	I see the value in personal-ization, but struggle with execution	I consistently create experiences that make customers feel valued
Hospitality as a Business Mindset	I don't consider hospitality in marketing	I acknowledge its value, but don't always apply it	I actively use hospitality principles in all customer interactions

Reflection Questions:

- Do you create marketing strategies that genuinely make customers feel special?
- Have you embraced hospitality as an essential business mindset, not just for hospitality brands?

Final Reflection

What shifts in thinking have you noticed as you progressed through the book?

Where might you still need to improve?

How will you apply these concepts moving forward in your marketing career?

Next Steps

Revisit chapters where you scored lower to reinforce learning.

Continue evolving your marketing mindset beyond the book by staying engaged with industry trends.

Apply hospitality-driven marketing principles in your business, regardless of industry.

This scorecard has guided you to think strategically, act with intent, and embrace a hospitality-driven marketing mindset. As you move forward, continue refining your approach, applying what you've learned, and staying open to new insights. Keep growing, keep learning, and, most importantly, keep marketing with purpose.

Acknowledgments

This book was inspired by my students and the joy I have teaching in college classrooms. Thank you to all the students who sat through my courses as an adjunct at New York University, a visiting professor at ESSEC in France, and a full-time faculty member at Boston University's School of Hospitality. I've learned from each of you.

I particularly love those "lightbulb moments" (as I enthusiastically refer to them) when I see a student "getting it," when they clearly demonstrate a sudden "ah-hah" micro-moment, and my lessons click. What is just as rewarding is when a student reaches out, perhaps years after they graduate, and sends a note because something that happened at work reminded them of a lesson we learned together or a situation from our class together. I treasure those instances. As I tried sitting down numerous times to document my thoughts for this personal souvenir of a book, I thought of so many of my students with whom I'm still in touch. #proudprofessor

I've had the remarkable gift of collaborating with the extraordinary students at Boston University's School of Hospitality Administration for over a decade now. Throughout this period at BU, countless seniors and graduate students have stood out. Many initially approached the challenge of marketing with skepticism, only to discover a profound appreciation for its intricate blend of critical thinking and tangible results. Witnessing their growth has been immensely rewarding. Time and again, I've encountered students who showcased exceptional savvy and demonstrated a keen understanding of the methodologies and creativity vital to any business endeavor, particularly in the realm of hospitality, and with an understanding of the nuances of strategic and digital marketing. I just love my students. They really are amazing.

Even more rewarding for me is the ongoing connection I maintain with so many of them. They have since flourished into successful professionals within the hospitality industry or hospitality-adjacent fields. I smile when they reach out with anecdotes recalling lessons from our classes, sometimes spanning years back, triggered by experiences in their workplaces or encounters with advertisements or commercials that provoke thought. I'm endlessly grateful to these individuals as our friendships endure. We continue to connect, share insights, and learn from each other, fostering a relationship far beyond the classroom. They are now my industry colleagues. I encourage them to call me by my first name, which isn't easy for them to do, and I understand.

I was also fortunate to have an experience teaching French hospitality graduate students at the ESSEC Business School in Cergy, France. I learned a great deal simply because of the cultural nuances of interaction in a classroom environment. I taught Strategic Marketing and Digital Marketing, and six rockstar students braved taking two consecutive days of six-hour-long sessions with me by registering for both classes (merci to Alban Sucrot, Johanna Reboullet, Eugénie Foucher, Laurie Moreau, Harsh Gohite, and Aliénor Argüello). We shared the same passions for marketing and hospitality, and the mutual respect and admiration will last with me. Thank you to the ESSEC students who contributed stories and lessons learned for this book. Merci beaucoup.

Thank You

I have enjoyed working closely with six students who served as my teaching assistants at Boston University over the years. They know me so well and have retained their amazing marketing mindsets today. Thank you, Elise Borkan Mackin, Kim Kibler, Marut Raval, Lawrence Mannix, Mackenzie Miers, and Paulina Preciat.

Thank you to the former students who willingly replied to my emails to share their reflections in this book. Many here are BU graduates; some are ESSEC grads. While it was impossible to include everyone's submission, I appreciate your contributions and continued connection. Names below are included throughout the pages of this book. (Stay tuned for Book 2 and more student contributions.)

Amin Adjmi, John Barton, Chloe Brendlinger, Samantha Cooper, Parker Doyle, Vivian Feinstein-Gough, Eugénie Foucher, Celina Friedman, Harsh Gohite, Mingjing He, Theresa Hughes, Clare Jun, Eva Kapoor, Raegan Kelly, Kimberly Kibler, Teagan Lucchese, Elise Borkan Macklin, Lawrence Mannix, Corinne Ognibene, Josh Ohebshalom, Richard Peet Hanna, Thi Thu Hang Nguyen, Marut Raval, Johanna Reboullet, Mai S., Hoda Sherdy, Victoria Textoris, Lucas Topper, Jovanna Fazzinni Tracz, Kaitlyn Tran, and Micaela Yee.

I must also extend gratitude to the BU School of Hospitality and acknowledge our esteemed academic journal, the *Boston Hospitality Review*, for permission to republish the Q&As I had assembled in the April and May 2024 *Marketing Innovation* editions. These conversations share insights from professional marketers whom I deeply admire; some of whom are also active members and advocates of HSMAI, the Hospitality Sales and Marketing Association International:

Roger Drake of Drake PR for his energizing contributions.

Julie Freeman of MMGY Global for her highly respected expertise and foresight on the future of public relations.

Michael Goldrich of Vivander Associates for his thought-provoking contributions (and serving as my AI "spirit guru").

Dylan Huey of REACH for his innovation and forward-thinking approach to the profession of influencers.

Marc Mazodier of the ESSEC Business School in Cergy, France, for his exceptional accomplishments and the kindness he and his wine connoisseur wife showed me while I was teaching in Paris.

Pete Rosenblum, founder of Map360, for his ever creative and straightforward insights; Pete and his team do amazing big-ticket activations and work. They are all WOW moments.

Adam Wallace, the visionary founder and CEO of Spherical, has hired several of my former digital marketing students. I'm so pleased the course has provided a pipeline for his agency's talent.

Thank you to my incredible friends in the business who represent the hotels, restaurants, festivals, agencies, food halls, culinary programs, spas, attractions, and hospitality services that have supported and continue to motivate our students in Boston (and in Paris). These opportunities enabled us to "peek under the sheets" and see what's really happening. We were able to learn in real time and help build the students' resumes with extraordinary experiences. These projects have led to the implementation of the students' ideas, letters of recommendation, and even internship and job offers. The students are fortunate to pursue an industry where veterans are eager to share and encourage the next generation of hospitality and marketing professionals. I'm honored to facilitate those classroom conversations and moments.

It's too difficult to name all the industry friends who have contributed to my classes, but I have to share a special shout-out to Marianna Accomando, Joe Mellia, Efren Aponte, Passion Smith, Seth Gerber, Andy Husbands, Candice Beaulieau, Sean Leonard, David Gibbons, and Martha Sheridan—who opened their doors to us more than once because of the trust they put in my classes and the confidence they have in our students and their bright minds.

I would like to extend heartfelt gratitude to my former students from the Class of 2025—Allie Rho, Emily Sands, Makayla Surette, and Emma Bogursky—for their invaluable feedback and support in reviewing various chapters of this book. And a really *loud* shout out to Charlotte Cook, who enthusiastically read chapters, shared feedback, and endured the arduous task of helping me edit to ensure a (hopefully) user-friendly book size and easy read. Charlotte, you are wonderful.

Thank you, Mike Oshins (Z"L), my big brother who mentored me when I started teaching. I miss you every day and having Zach in my class was a blessing. Maybe he felt a tinge of you through my teaching style in the classroom. BDE.

A heartfelt thank you to my loving family, Alain, Jordy, Zach, and Jeremy, for whom I work so hard in hopes of making you proud. I love you all so much. And to the everlasting, immortal Charli, who loyally sat, lay, and begged for food beside me as I furiously typed away at these chapters. It's because I miss you so much that I was determined to finish this book—and the next one. You are forever in our hearts, you silly little girl. Always our puppy.

Resources and References

Chapter 1: Think Like a Marketer. Act Like an Owner.

American Marketing Association. n.d. *American Marketing Association*. https://www.ama.org

Merriam-Webster. n.d. *Merriam-Webster Dictionary*. https://www.merriam-webster.com

Lanz, Leora. 2024. "Insights into Marketing: An Interview with Professor Marc Mazodier." *Boston Hospitality Review*, April. https://www.bu.edu/bhr

Chapter 2: What's Your Why?

Sinek, Simon. 2009. *Start with Why: How Great Leaders Inspire Everyone to Take Action*. New York: Portfolio.

Chouinard, Yvon. 2011. "Patagonia: Don't Buy This Jacket." *Harvard Business Review*. https://hbr.org

Mycoskie, Blake. 2011. *Start Something That Matters*. New York: Spiegel and Grau.Freedman, Jill. 2017. "What's Your Brand Story?" TED video, December. https://www.ted.com

Chapter 3: The Brand and the Experience

Batat, Wided. 2020. *Experiential Marketing: Consumer Behavior, Customer Experience, and the 7Es*. London: Routledge.

Kotler, Philip, and Kevin Lane Keller. 2016. *Marketing Management*. 15th ed. Boston: Pearson.

Lanz, Leora. 2024. "Insights into Marketing: An Interview with Julie Freeman." *Boston Hospitality Review*, March. https://www.bu.edu/bhr

Cvent. 2020. "6 Must-See Examples of Personalized Hotel Marketing." *Cvent Blog*, April. https://www.cvent.com/en/blog/hospitality/personalized-hotel-marketing

Lecinski, Jim. 2011. *Winning the Zero Moment of Truth*. Vook, Inc.

Moseley Group. n.d. *Moseley Group*. https://moseley.group

Stone, Brad. 2013. *The Everything Store: Jeff Bezos and the Age of Amazon*. New York: Little,

Brown and Company. Hasbro. n.d. "Play-Doh: The Story Behind the Brand." https://www.playdoh.com/en-us/about-us/ McDonald, Kevin, and Daniel Smith-Rowsey. 2016.

"The Netflix Effect: Technology and Entertainment in the 21st Century." *Media, Culture and Society* 38 (4): 564–577. https://doi.org/10.1177/0163443716631704 Turner, Andrew W. 2019.

Starbucks: A History of the Company. Austin, TX: Greenleaf Book Group Press. Baker, Sara. 2018. "Airbnb: The New Face of Travel." *Harvard Business School*. https://www.hbs.edu/faculty/Pages/item.aspx?num=51578

Chapter 4: Brand Extensions and Positioning for Growth

Villa-Clarke, Angelina. 2024. "Inside the Rise of the Fashion x Luxury Hotels Relationship." *Forbes*, March 27. https://www.forbes.com/sites/angelinavillaclarke/2024/03/27/

Woods, Rachel. 2021. "TGI Fridays Expands Frozen Food Line to Grocery Stores." *QSR Magazine*. https://www.qsrmagazine.com/news/tgi-fridays-expands-frozen-food-line-grocery-stores

Villa-Clarke, Angelina. 2021. "Inside the Luxury of the New Cheval Blanc Hotel in Paris."

Forbes, July 12. https://www.forbes.com/sites/angelinavillaclarke/2021/07/12/

Lyons Group. n.d. "About Us." *Lyons Group*. https://www.lyonsgroup.com/

Mistral Bistro. n.d. "Welcome to Our Restaurant." Accessed January 27, 2025. https://mistralbistro.com/

Jenkins, Amanda. 2016. "How Red Bull and GoPro's Partnership Changed the Game for Extreme Sports." *Adweek*, October 10. https://www.adweek.com/creativity/how-red-bull-and-gopros-partnership-changed-game-extreme-sports-173203/

Gallo, Amber. 2020. "How Apple and Nike Are Changing the Game with Their Partnership." *Forbes*, December 14. https://www.forbes.com/sites/ambergallo/2020/12/14/

Lindsay, Kyle. 2022. "Warby Parker and Arby's Partnership Is a Feast for the Eyes." *Ad Age*, March 2. https://adage.com/article/marketing/warby-parker-arbys-partnership-feast-eyes/2322566

Schachter, Ken. 2018. "Northwell Health Rebrands with a New Look and Message." *Newsday*, January 10. https://www.newsday.com/business/northwell-health-rebrands-1.15717431

Lott, Dawn. 2021. "Mercure Hotels Embraces Chatbot Technology for Guest Personalization." *Hotel Management*, October 5. https://www.hotelmanagement.net/technology/mercure-hotels-embraces-chatbot-technology-guest-personalization

Glassdoor. n.d. "Employer Branding 101: Why, How and Proven ROI." *Glassdoor for Employers*. https://www.glassdoor.com/employers/resources/employer-branding-101-why-how-and-proven-roi/

Chapter 5: Start with the End Goals

American Marketing Association. n.d. "Cost per Goal Planning." Accessed January 27, 2025. https://www.ama.org/ Moorman, Christine, and George S. Day. 2016. "Organizing for Marketing Excellence." *Journal of Marketing* 80 (6): 1–18. https://doi.org/10.1509/jm.80.6.1

Chapter 6: Transactions to Trust: Building Relationships

Row 34. n.d. *Row 34*. https://www.row34.com/

Lanz, Leora. 2024. "Insights into Marketing: An Interview with Julie Freeman." *Boston Hospitality Review*, April. https://www.bu.edu/bhr

Punch Bowl Brookline. n.d. *Punch Bowl Brookline.*
https://www.punchbowlbrookline.com/

Chapter 7: The Brand of You

Spurlock, Morgan. 2011. "The Greatest TED Talk Ever
Sold." TED video, February. https://www.youtube.com/
watch?v=R7n4xV3sI7U

Chapter 8: Stay Current, Relevant, Connected

Lanz, Leora. 2024. "Insights into Marketing: An
Interview with Dylan Huey." *Boston Hospitality Review*,
May. https://www.bu.edu/bhr

Lanz, Leora. 2024. "Insights into Marketing: An
Interview with Adam Wallace." *Boston Hospitality
Review*, May. https://www.bu.edu/bhr

Joseph, J. 2020. *The Conscious Marketer: Inspiring
a Deeper and More Conscious Brand Experience.*
Washington, DC: Amplify Publishing Group.

Gallo, Carmine. 2014. *Talk Like TED: The 9
Public-Speaking Secrets of the World's Top Minds.* New
York: St. Martin's Press.

Sinek, Simon. 2011. *Start with Why: How Great Leaders
Inspire Everyone to Take Action.* New York: Penguin
Group.

Chapter 9: Marketing for the Future: Innovation, Sustainability, and Social Impact

Lanz, Leora. 2024. "Insights into Marketing: An Interview with Roger Drake." *Boston Hospitality Review*, May. https://www.bu.edu/bhr

Lanz, Leora. 2024. "Insights into Marketing: An Interview with Adam Wallace." *Boston Hospitality Review*, May. https://www.bu.edu/bhr

Witt Certified. n.d. *Witt Certified*. https://www.wittcertified.com/

Lanz, Leora. 2024. "Insights into Marketing: An Interview with Julie Freeman." *Boston Hospitality Review*, March. https://www.bu.edu/bhr

Lanz, Leora. 2024. "Insights into Marketing: An Interview with Sandra King." *Boston Hospitality Review*, April. https://www.bu.edu/bhr

Chapter 10: Remember the Hospitality

Chewy. n.d. "Operating Principles." *Chewy Careers*. Accessed January 28, 2025. https://careers.chewy.com/us/en/operating-principles

Meyer, Danny. 2006. *Setting the Table: The Transforming Power of Hospitality in Business*. New York: HarperCollins.

Guidara, Will. 2022. *Unreasonable Hospitality: The Remarkable Power of Giving People More Than They Expect.* New York: HarperCollins.

Endnotes

1   Build it and they will come. Is it a myth? Occasionally, I hear about a business or an entrepreneur who prides themselves in "not spending on marketing" or "advertising." They credit their exceptional service to drive word-of-mouth for future bookings or business. I say, these are rare breed businesses, and that's awesome if that can sustain long-term success. But for service businesses that are in a greatly competitive space, not investing in any form of marketing to any persona in your market mix will backfire. The hope is that exclusive word-of-mouth (WOM) can lead to online or "digital" word-of-mouth (DWOM), and if your voice is not engaging with the online conversation that is in place (ORM = online reputation management), readers will think you do not care, and that will backfire.

2   What is a travel or destination "dupe?" Dupes refer to lesser-known destinations that are not as famous or "mainstream" as their counterparts but often just as culturally rich and beautiful. It has been the increasing expense of travel, which emerged thanks to pent-up demand after the global pandemic, that has led individuals who are so eager to experience the world to find alternative destinations.

These alternatives do not (yet) suffer from overtourism, are more affordable, and are likely still beautifully raw and untouched by heavy development.

3 "Greenwashing" is the term for communicating an embellished or unsubstantiated claim to deceive consumers. It refers to the information shared that leads people into believing a company's products are environmentally friendly or have a greater positive environmental impact than they actually do.

4 By the way, Harley Davidson is a terrific example of a company that can project the needs, desires, and changes in its customers to periodically reposition itself, which it has done over the years rather successfully: either shifting from a brand of "defiance" to "lifestyle," from mass market to niche, and recognizing when it's time to reach a new generation of customer to stay relevant for the future. Harley Davidson understands that when customers share their 'why,' they are more apt to serve as brand ambassadors and champions.

5 A meta description is a short snippet of text (typically 150–160 characters) that summarizes the content of a web page. It helps users determine if they should review the site or not. Google wants web developers to create and use meta descriptions.

6 My brand is defined by a passion for hospitality and a commitment to inspiring young people to pursue it with love and dedication. I believe in lifting others while uplifting myself, fostering an environment where mutual trust and support thrive. By connecting friends from around the world, I create a network of meaningful and lasting relationships built on trust and collaboration. Yet, in the classroom, I am firm. I have high standards, and

sometimes even higher expectations, and I want the students to have an amazing experience class to class. So, meeting these standards is imperative. I credit my mom for raising me with a spirit of tough love. I push my students to "go a bit further" in every action they take. I want them to dig deeper, and they will learn more and learn better. As Pierre Lego, one of my students at ESSEC told me, "I enjoyed the material even more because I was inspired to dig deeper and perform better." In this realm of tough love, I know that our students will make a positive impact in the global hospitality community, with our personal connections, and in society in general.

7   REACH is a national collegiate organization dedicated to empowering student content creators, digital marketers, and aspiring influencers by providing the tools, experiences, and connections needed to succeed in the professional world.

8   We touched on "owned" media earlier in our chapters. "Owned, earned, and paid media" represent how a brand distributes content. Owned media includes channels the brand controls (its website or email list), earned media refers to publicity gained through word of mouth or public relations (reviews or media coverage), and paid media involves advertising the brand pays for (social ads or sponsored content).

9   An advertorial is a piece of content that looks like an objective editorial, but it is in fact a paid promotional piece. It must be identified as "sponsored content." Affiliate marketing is a performance based approach where a business rewards third party 'affiliates' who drive traffic or sales to that business. For example, if a travel blogger promotes a hotel, and the reader clicks on that blogger's affiliate link and books a room, the blogger will earn a commission.

About the Author

Some people map out their careers with precision, but mine has been guided by a willingness to embrace opportunities and a deep belief that happiness matters more than anything else. Financial success was never my primary driver; I focused on creating value for others and finding joy in my work. It was the satisfaction of contributing alongside individuals I respect in an industry I love that mattered most. For me, it's about the experiences, the people, and the trust built along the way. It's also about self-respect and integrity.

My journey in hospitality began in high school with a summer internship on the hospitality training team for the now-shuttered restaurant brand, Beefsteak Charlie's.

Does anyone remember the all-you-can-eat salad bar and the all-you-can-drink sodas? I had so much fun learning about service and making employees and customers happy. Throughout college, my "work-study" financial aid job was as a server, host, busser, and stock person at an on-campus restaurant, where I enjoyed the team synergy that created a beautifully choreographed flow of service.

During graduate school, I held two internships simultaneously—one with the newly opened Four Seasons Hotel on the Boston Common and the other with the city's destination marketing agency (the latter thanks to a successful group project from school). Those experiences shaped my understanding of hospitality and the power of relationships. Years later, former mentors from the Four Seasons called me with an opportunity that changed everything: a move from Boston to New York City, where I took on marketing and branding challenges I never could have imagined.

Leading public relations efforts for the rebranding and repositioning of the ITT Sheraton Hotels of New York City was an incredible learning experience. Working daily with sales and operations colleagues, managing crises, and occasionally engaging with VIPs and celebrities taught me the nuances of marketing communication and the importance of working "on property."

After nearly a decade in New York, I spent fifteen years at the global hospitality consulting firm HVS as the Global Director of Marketing and Communications.

For fourteen of those years, I also wore two hats, spearheading the marketing efforts for clients in the Americas and the Caribbean. I managed branding, social media, and conference marketing while advising hotel owners and hospitality services. I later launched LHL Communications, helping hotels, restaurants, and tourism organizations sharpen their branding and digital strategies through content creation, storytelling, and strategic consulting.

Perhaps the biggest surprise of my career has been teaching. What started as a temporary gig at Boston University's School of Hospitality Administration evolved into a long-term relationship, proving that unexpected turns can lead to fabulous new destinations. As an Associate Professor of the Practice, I developed and teach courses on Experiential Marketing and Hospitality Digital Marketing Strategies. Working with students eager to shape the future of hospitality is both inspiring and humbling. I've developed a reputation for "tough love" in the classroom, setting high expectations while nurturing their growth and success.

My teaching experiences shaped this book, which explores the principles behind a hospitality-driven marketing mindset, encouraging critical and strategic thinking. In the follow-up to this book, *Marketing Mindset in Motion: Inspired by Hospitality*, we build on that foundation, furthering practical applications, sharing real-world examples, and highlighting technical approaches to thinking like a marketer.

I strive to give back to the industry that has given me so much. I am a founding board member of the non-profit Center for Responsible Hospitality and a member of the International Society of Hospitality Consultants and the Hospitality Sales & Marketing Association International. I've been honored to serve on HSMAI's Americas Advisory Board and recognized as one of the Top 100 Powerful Leaders in Hospitality and one of the Top Influential Hospitality Educators in 2022, 2023, and 2024 by the International Hospitality Institute.

Beyond work, I enjoy spring, summer, and fall mornings at the beach with a good book in hand. Biographies enable me to learn people's stories; fiction set in Paris (where I've been blessed with two brief teaching stints) transports me; and food or travel writing lifts my spirit. I treasure Long Island's East End beaches, food tours around the world, and collecting gems and shells. I'm also a passionate advocate for sustainable tourism, koala conservation, and enjoying long walks with friends, especially by the ocean.

Most of all, I am grateful—grateful for my family, my students, my friends, and my industry colleagues. I cherish the relationships, mentorship, and inspiration shared with hospitality professionals across Boston, New York, Paris, and in the many places around the world where I've been so blessed to participate in the business of hospitality.